UNION CINEMAS RITZ

A STORY OF THEATRE ORGANS AND CINE-VARIETY

DONALD INKSTER

THE WICK

UNION CINEMAS RITZ

A STORY OF THEATRE ORGANS
AND CINE-VARIETY

First published by The Wick Book Publishers
PO Box 2257, Hove, East Sussex BN3 1NQ
England.
1999

A catalogue record of this book
is available from the British Library

ISBN 0 9533993 9 7

Format & design by StewART

Printed and bound by
Smart Litho, Brighton, England.

For Françoise

CONTENTS

AUTHOR'S NOTE AND ACKNOWLEDGEMENTS

The inspiration for this book came from a series of articles about Union Cinemas which I wrote for Theatre Organ Review and which appeared quarterly in that journal for a period running from March 1957 to March 1958. These amounted to little more than a brief outline of the activities of the company during its heyday, with particular reference to cinemas equipped with organs and provision for stage shows. I myself had visited the flagship Union Cinema in Kingston upon Thames several times in 1937 and had gathered together a considerable amount of material in the form of cuttings from the national and local press, the BBC's Radio Times and commercial radio's Radio Pictorial. To this was added additional information obtained from provincial newspapers all over the country, together with trade magazines such as Kinematograph Weekly, Ideal Kinema and Cinema and Theatre Construction, carefully perused in the course of visits to the National Newspaper Library at Colindale. I liaised closely with Frank Hare, Northern Secretary of the Theatre Organ Club, who acted as editor of the articles and supplied many of the illustrations. The series appeared to be well received, which made all the work of preparation worth while.

Over the years that followed I continued to pay visits to the British Newspaper Library in the course of my researches and I wrote many other articles, almost always on cinema and theatre organ topics, these appearing for the most part in Theatre Organ Review and The Cinema Organ Society Journal. I also wrote letters on similar topics which regularly appeared in the correspondence columns of such journals as The Organ, Musical Opinion and Organists' Review.

Inevitably, in the course of dealing with other subjects, I found myself picking up more and more material relating to Union Cinemas and in due course the idea struck me that perhaps I should attempt a full-length book on the subject. It would offer a fairly comprehensive history of the growth and development of the circuit, including financial matters, but particular emphasis would be laid upon the promotion of theatre organ music, stage shows and live entertainment generally, as this became such an important part of company policy and the main reason for which it is best remembered. Once I had made the decision to proceed I naturally set to work with renewed vigour. It involved going back over old ground as well as breaking into much that was new in order to achieve the degree of comprehensiveness I believed the project warranted. What follows is the result.

For the benefit of readers who may be unfamiliar with the old pre-decimal currency, the pound used to be divided into twenty shillings and the shillings into twelve pence. With the introduction of the decimal currency the pound was divided into one hundred pence. As an example, a share price quoted as £8.15s.0d. would now be shown as £8.75.

ACKNOWLEDGEMENTS

In addition to the journals mentioned above, my researches at the British Newspaper Library over a period of more than forty years have covered literally dozens of newspapers and periodicals and I am extremely grateful to the Library personnel for all their assistance.

Concerning the illustrations, the aim has been to present views of some of the important cinemas in the chain, a number of typical organ consoles, members of the Union team of organists and a selection of advertisement blocks taken from the national and local press.

Almost all of the photographs have been in existence for many years and most have appeared elsewhere - some of them on numerous occasions. I was particularly anxious to ensure that the organists should be shown at Union consoles, so all these obviously date from the 1930's. I would have liked to have included Pierson Webber and Gordon Banner but I had no success in tracking anything down. Some of the interior and exterior views of cinemas are more recent, as are those of organ consoles, but nevertheless they are already several decades old. I have found it extremely difficult to establish ownership of copyright. In some instances more than one individual has claimed ownership of the same photograph, while in others the identity of the original photographer appears to have been lost altogether. In these circumstances I have felt that my best course of action has been simply to state from whose collection each photograph has been taken and I trust that readers will be happy with this arrangement.

I am equally indebted to so many friends for their interest in the project and for their help and encouragement. These include Neville Meale, Dudley Savage, Arthur Lord, Nigel Ogden, Len Rawle, Simon Gledhill, Richard Cole, Frank Hare, Eric Atkin, Basil Bonner, John D. Sharp, Ian MacNaught, Tim Moody, John Leeming, Ivor Buckingham and Quentin Bellamy. I especially thank my old friend Tony Moss for his outstanding input and support throughout the preparation of this book for which I am most grateful. In particular I wish to thank him for the loan of the souvenir programme of the opening of the Regal, Kingston, extracts from which appear as Appendix One. I hope that I have not left anyone out!

INTRODUCTION
SUPER CINEMAS & CINE-VARIETY

For the most part, books about the cinema have to do with films and film-making rather than the places where they are exhibited. Literature dealing with the development of the "picture palace" does certainly exist, though in appreciably smaller quantities. My own researches have yielded relatively little in the way of published histories of the growth and development of the major cinema chains which took place between the two World Wars, more especially following the advent of the "talkies" at the end of the 1920's. Here and there one may find occasional references to cinema provision in books dealing with local history. In more recent years, however, many of those cinemas have been closed down, in some instances being demolished and in others being adapted for other uses such as bingo halls. Those remaining open have usually been converted into smaller units housing two or three screens: forerunners of the current purpose-built multiplex cinemas offering a wide selection of feature films simultaneously - but very little else.

The days of palatial, richly-decorated auditoria in which films, live musical interludes, elaborate stage presentations and even talent contests were regularly presented - Cine-Variety in fact - are long gone and have never been experienced by new generations of cinemagoers.

The whole ethos of film presentation has indeed undergone a radical change. An important consequence of this has been a wave of nostalgia for the heady days of the "super cinema" and the all-round entertainment it provided. In the United Kingdom important work is now being performed by such organisations as The Cinema Theatre Association in securing preservation orders on appropriate cinema buildings and publishing books dealing comprehensively with the development of major circuits, packed full of information and profusely illustrated. One thinks of such concerns as ABC (Associated British Cinemas), Gaumont-British, Odeon, Granada and so on, all of which were actively engaged in the construction of new cinemas. These were sited not only in town and city centres but often in suburban areas where new housing estates called for the provision of shopping parades, banks, places of worship and of course places of entertainment. This activity accelerated in the 1930's and continued right up to the outbreak of war in the summer of 1939, with a number of outstanding projects completed during the early years of the war.

Others, too, have written in similar vein. In addition, the various theatre organ clubs and societies are also concerned with preservation, since these places were originally the true home of these specialised instruments and remain cherished as such, although many of the organs themselves now reside elsewhere.

It has to be remembered that in those days, when television was still in its infancy, cinema-going was one of the most important leisure activities available, weekly visits being commonplace and two or even three visits per week being by no means unusual. In such a climate, cinema construction was big business and a number of distinguished architects of the period specialised in this field.

The new "super cinemas", once opened, were strongly promoted, with great emphasis on showmanship. Performances were almost invariably continuous and of seldom less than three hours' duration. In addition to the main feature film, which would usually run for 80-90 minutes, there would be a second feature film (nowadays sometimes referred to as a "B-movie") running for around 60 minutes. The remaining time would be taken up by a newsreel, together with additional short items: a cartoon or a general interest film such as a travelogue. If, as was often the case, a theatre organ was installed, an interlude of live music would be provided. The organ, originally conceived for the accompaniment of silent films, was featured as a solo instrument in its own right and was often played by organists who had achieved "star" status by reason of regular broadcasts and recording contracts. Thus was provided live entertainment to relieve the impersonal projection of images upon the screen. Many of the larger cinemas went further and presented lavish stage shows as well, thus supplying a mixture of film and live performance - often referred to as "Cine-Variety" and featuring leading singers, dancers, comedians and speciality acts. Musical accompaniment when needed would as a rule be provided by the organist, though occasionally an orchestra might be featured. From time to time one of the leading broadcasting dance bands would be the main attraction. Live entertainment was often strongly promoted, never more so than by Union Cinemas.

Admission prices to cinemas were remarkably affordable, ranging from only 6d. or 9d. to 2s.6d. or 3s.0d. in most cases, although in the West End of London they tended to be somewhat higher as befitted this location, plus the fact that most first releases of new films took place there. The value for money represented by the entertainment on offer was often quite outstanding and full houses were commonplace. Indeed, "Standing room only" and "Queue here" signs were very much a part of the necessary equipment of the cinema. Such was the demand that in a good many instances plans for the auditorium would include special provision for a given number of standees.

In this book I have attempted to describe the history of Union Cinemas, a company which assumed major importance during this period but which, for various reasons, failed to survive. From its beginnings in June 1928 the company at first expanded by means of acquisitions of individual cinemas and existing small chains, soon to embark on a programme of new construction. As well as seeking to provide modern cinemas in towns which previously did not have them, an important part of the policy was to acquire as many as possible of the existing halls in the towns where they established a presence, in order to achieve superior bargaining power in negotiating film rentals.

Union Cinemas also adopted a policy of really heavy promotion of the theatre organ and stage shows to supplement the film programme. Broadcasts by the leading organists were standard fare during the 1930's, but these were soon followed by variety shows on both BBC and commercial radio, with personal appearances by many of the most famous artistes of those days - all this in addition to the film programmes.

Unfortunately, for various reasons, Union Cinemas ran into financial difficulties resulting in the resignation of all the directors at the end of October 1937. The circumstances leading to this situation became generally known during the months which followed, when the management of the Associated British Picture Corporation had acquired control of the bulk of the circuit and had conducted a full investigation into the affairs of the company. The report which followed in due course shed much light upon the way in which these affairs had been conducted and I have devoted considerable space to it, stating the facts and figures exactly as published at the time and without adopting a judgmental stance.

In retrospect it is sad to reflect on the relatively short history of Union Cinemas; one can only speculate as to what further advances might have been made in other circumstances, or as to what might have occurred had another of the major cinema chains taken over control. But there can be no denying those exciting days of 1936-37 when the Company's progress had reached its peak: new cinemas opening almost weekly, broadcasts of organ music and variety shows almost daily, regular press releases and advertisements and so on. What a pity it all had to end. I have endeavoured to trace the development of all these activities, using contemporary sources of information as well as personal recollections, and hope that by placing them on record in this form I shall have successfully achieved my purpose.

CHAPTER ONE

THE DRIVING FORCE

The period during which Union Cinemas is best remembered for its cinema-building programme and its strong promotion of Cine-Variety is 1936-37, but in order to view its activities in those years in proper perspective I believe it is desirable to give an account of the company's development from its earliest days and of what followed afterwards.

The driving force behind the creation and development of Union Cinemas was a businessman named David Bernhard. Born in Bradford in 1861, he entered the wool trade and for some years travelled extensively as a salesman in the Far East. He enjoyed considerable success, securing record orders for wool and building up a sizeable fortune in the process. After returning to England he acquired the wool firm of Charles Seman & Co. Ltd., becoming chairman and in due course establishing himself as one of the most prominent figures in the industry at that time. In 1919 he decided to retire and moved south to take up residence in Shirley, near Croydon.

In the years following the Great War of 1914-1918 David Bernhard recognised the potential of films and film-making: he financed British Exhibitors Films Ltd., registered in 1922, and appointed one of his sons, Charles Frederick Bernhard, as Managing Director. A separate enterprise, Bernhard-Tiffany Productions, was then established in 1924 to produce a series of special films. Following a visit to America, an amalgamation was arranged whereby B.E.F.would become distributors for the ongoing film output - some twelve short films in the first year of operation, doubling to twenty-four in the second. John M. Stahl, an outstanding producer in the USA, was recruited to run this side of the business.

14

Meanwhile, work had started in 1927 on what it was hoped would be the first "talkie" to be shown in this country - "To What Red Hell" - starring Sybil Thorndike, but owing to unforeseen problems and delays it was eventually beaten into second place by "Blackmail", Alfred Hitchcock's first sound film.

David Bernhard quickly realised that talking pictures would revolutionise the film industry, with cinema entertainment outperforming even live theatre, and he decided to shift his attention to cinemas themselves. He therefore floated the Union Cinema Co. Ltd. in 1928, acquiring seven existing cinemas and the whole of the issued capital of B.E.F. and Bernhard-Tiffany Productions. It would seem that initially the object was to produce films and acquire cinemas to exhibit them on an exclusive basis, but with the advent of the first "talkies" the decision was taken to leave the film production side completely in order to concentrate solely on the development of a chain of cinemas which in due course could be expanded to cover the whole country.

The Union Cinema Co. Ltd. was registered on 18 June 1928 with a capital of £300,000 in the form of 800,000 10% cumulative preference shares of 5s. each and 2,000,000 ordinary shares of 1s. each. The official notice announced its purpose as being "to carry on the business of proprietors or managers of theatres, palaces, halls, buildings, grounds or places for kinematograph shows, etc." The directors named were Frederick Bernhard, J.Davies Harries, S.J.Flateau and L.J.Clements.

The first seven cinemas acquired were from companies operated by L.J.Clements and N.D.Fitzgerald and were:

Grand, Huddersfield
Victoria Hall, Portsmouth
Adelaide, Newcastle upon Tyne
St. James's, King's Lynn
Electric, King's Lynn
Rialto, Maidenhead
Picture Theatre, Maidenhead

Thus began the lengthy process of developing the chain of cinemas, initially by the acquisition of existing halls. Several of them were old and it was accepted that as more were added to the group there would be scope for reconstruction and refurbishment in certain cases to produce something more in keeping with modern requirements. The

Picture Theatre at Maidenhead was presently dealt with in this way. In due course, with the establishment of a viable base and the prospect of raising additional capital by means of new share issues, it would become possible to embark on an ambitious programme of new construction.

The process of acquisition continued and by the end of 1930 the following cinemas had been added to the chain:

Plaza, Maidenhead	Empire, King's Lynn
Regal, Bath	Majestic, Newcastle
Alexandra, Southampton	PictureTheatre, Winchester
Picture Theatre, Woolston	

At the beginning of June 1931 it was announced that three additional halls had been acquired in Oxford: the Electra, the Super and the George Street Cinema, effectively giving the Company complete control of the town's cinemas. It became ongoing Union policy to arrive at this situation in as many places as possible, thereby strengthening the Company's bargaining power in the matter of film rentals.

This gave a total of seventeen cinemas in the circuit. The Super at Oxford boasted an early Spurdon Rutt organ and the Plaza, Maidenhead had a small Wurlitzer, but little use was being made of either of them and there was as yet no policy of featuring the organ. It would not be long before such a policy was introduced, however, as the entertainment value of the organ interlude as promoted elsewhere was quickly recognised.

For a while, the progress of Union Cinemas was somewhat slow and profits tended to be meagre - mainly due to the competition from other cinemas. However, following the acquisition of the Public Hall, Gravesend, the first really major work of modernisation was carried out there to plans drawn up by the company's house architect, A.H.Jones, ARIBA.

Originally the entrance had been through a rather narrow passage, but by acquiring the adjacent premises it was possible to create a much more attractive entrance hall. The paybox was situated in the centre, complete with its electrically operated ticket-issuing machines supplied by the aptly-named Automaticket Ltd. Doors to the stalls were located on either side and access to the balcony was by means of a central staircase. Structural alterations to the interior included raising the balcony itself in order to correct the sightlines from the rear stalls, setting back the projection room and extending the approach to the balcony around the side of the hall. These alterations made possible a significant increase the number of seats in the auditorium. The decorative scheme featured green, grey and black for the entrance hall, while beige picked out with silver was chosen for the auditorium, with beige upholstered seats on green carpeting and green and silver curtains with a backdrop also in beige. Outside, the frontage included a large canopy carrying illuminated announcements around the edge. There were also vertical neon signs showing the new name "Super" - visible up and down the main road.

The projection room was equipped with Kalee projectors, together with the latest Western Electric sound apparatus. A new Compton organ was installed, described as "mighty" but in reality quite small, being of 3 manuals (one of them a coupler manual having no speaking stops of its own but to which stops drawn on the other two manuals could be coupled at different pitches) and 5 pipe units. An illuminated glass console surround was fitted, this being of the "Cascade" type recently introduced by the electrical equipment firm F.H.Pride & Co. of Clapham, South London. The console itself was mounted on a lift situated in the centre of the orchestra pit. Finally, a popular personality in the district, Captain A.W.Rifkin, was appointed theatre manager.

The Opening Ceremony of the Super took place on Saturday 16 September 1933 and was preceded by a reception and dinner at the Royal Clarendon Hotel, Gravesend, at which Frederick Bernhard welcomed the special guests. These included the Mayor and Mayoress, the Town Clerk and a number of other local dignitaries. At the cinema the distinguished film actress Anna Neagle and her husband Herbert Wilcox, Director of Production for the British and Dominion Film Company, were guests of honour and received by the Theatre Controller, J.H.Lundy. Arc lamps had been set up on the canopy outside and in the foyer so that the arrival of the guests could be filmed for showing in the cinema the following week. The film programme included a newsreel, a new Walt Disney Silly Symphony and as the main feature the film "Cavalcade" - described as "The picture of the generation." The organ interlude was presented by Alex Taylor, one of the leading cinema organists at the time. He had gained experience in the USA and had returned to this country, appearing at several important openings (Davis', Croydon and the Granada, Tooting, to name but two). At Gravesend he was followed immediately by another well-known organist, Lewis Gerard, who joined Union Cinemas from the Orpheum, Golders Green. It could be said that this appointment marked the commencement of an organ policy. Live entertainment on the stage was also offered on a regular basis in addition to the film programme and after the opening of the Super the organ interlude was frequently supplemented or replaced by a stage show. "Olly Aston and his 1933 Band" appeared as early as week commencing 30 October, whilst for the week of 4 December "Jan Ralfini and his Famous Band - 18 players, direct from the New Victoria" (an important London cinema) were featured, followed one week later by "Younkman's Czardas Band" together with three variety acts. As a rule, the acts appearing in Cine-Variety included dancers, jugglers, impressionists and comedy double-acts of the kind which provided the bulk of the entertainment offered in music halls and variety theatres around the country, though from time to time top-of-the-bill artistes were signed up to make short tours of cinema circuits. As we shall see, Union Cinemas were destined to lead the field in promotions of this type.

During the year, negotiations were conducted leading to the amalgamation of the Union and Southan Morris circuits. William Southan Morris had worked in close association with the Bernhard family since the days of the B.E.F. and Bernhard-Tiffany organisations, but had worked independently to build up his own cinema chain. In retrospect, it would appear that for some time there had been a measure of co-operation between them, so that the eventual merger was not entirely unexpected. David Bernhard announced that it would not involve the formation of a new company or the raising of fresh capital. It transpired later that a consideration of £65,000 was paid to Southan Morris in respect of the merger. Cinemas involved in the arrangement included the following:

Palace, Banbury	Regal, Newbury
Super, Gravesend	Carlton, Newbury
Garrick, Hereford	Adelphi, Slough
Kemble, Hereford	Playhouse, Windsor
Empire, Luton	Royalty, Windsor
Plaza, Luton	Empire, Wolverton

The inclusion of the Super, Gravesend, in this list would appear to indicate that it had originally been part of the Southan Morris circuit, but the reconstruction and refurbishment was clearly the work of Union Cinemas and evidence of the merger to come. There was absolutely no mention of Southan Morris in the press reports of the reopening, all the credit being taken by Union, but I have a letter from Lewis Gerard stating that he was engaged as resident organist by none other than William Southan Morris himself!

As before, most of the cinemas were fairly old and of low seating capacity. Perhaps the most important, however, was the Adelphi, Slough, opened as recently as February 1930, a handsome structure with seating for 2,038 in the auditorium. A Christie organ of 3 manuals and 8 pipe units had been installed earlier in 1933 and opened by Bruce Wendell, a black organist who enjoyed considerable popularity at the time, having been resident at the Leicester Square Theatre in London's West End since June 1931.

The Playhouse, Windsor, was equipped with a small Compton organ of 2 manuals and 5 pipe units with an illuminated console of the "cascade" type. It had been opened in May 1933 by Edward O'Henry, another leading cinema organist with several "openings" to his credit. A graduate of the Royal Academy of Music, he was resident organist for two years at the Picture House, Walsall, which possessed the very first Wurlitzer organ to arrive in this country, and later spent a number of years at Tussaud's Cinema in London, from where he broadcast regularly and made a large number of records.

The press release concerning the amalgamation also stated that the number of cinemas owned or controlled by the Union Cinema Co. would now rise to over forty. Plans had been submitted for the construction of a 2,000-seat cinema at Tunbridge Wells and that sites had been acquired at Dartford, Newark and Southend. In addition, negotiations were said to be in hand for the acquisition of another group of cinemas. There was an element of optimism in this announcement, as the Tunbridge Wells cinema was opened as a 1,600-seater and nothing more was heard regarding the three sites. On the other hand, acquisitions did occur and at an accelerating pace in the months and years to come. Expansion was clearly the most important issue and press releases tended to be up-beat and prone to exaggeration.

Meanwhile, Lewis Gerard remained at the Super, Gravesend, until the end of the week commencing 5 February 1934 when he resigned from the Company. In a letter to me he felt that it had been a mistake to take up the appointment as the Super was a relatively small house and he had been happier at his previous post in Golders Green. He then returned to ABC (Associated British Cinemas) at the Empire, Coventry, followed by the Ritz, Leeds, from where he began regular

19

broadcasts. Later still he opened the enlarged organ in the rebuilt Dreamland Cinema in Margate - but that is another story. At Gravesend he was succeeded by Bruce Wendell who was billed "For a short season - direct from the Leicester Square Theatre." He remained until August, when it was announced that Alex Taylor had been appointed Musical Director for the company. The Super, Gravesend, was evidently still regarded as the flagship cinema of the Circuit and Taylor made his first appearance week commencing 20 August and remaining there until the opening of the new Tunbridge Wells cinema on 3 December 1934. He was then replaced by Neville Meale who was a nephew of Arthur Meale, the distinguished organist of the Central Hall, Westminster. At first he had trained as a concert organist and orchestral conductor, but turned to cinema work when he joined the Union Cinema Co.; he was to stay with them for several years.

In view of their close proximity, it was normal practice for the same organist to double between the Adelphi, Slough, and the Playhouse, Windsor. Initially, this was to be one who in due course would become a very popular member of the Union team: Frank Matthew. He, too, had had a sound classical training, having been a chorister at Durham Cathedral where he studied piano and organ under Dr. Armes, the cathedral organist. He later became interested in the cinema organ and opened the Wurlitzer at the Havelock Cinema, Sunderland, eventually broadcasting from there. He was the featured organist at several openings, including the Electric, Bournemouth, the Capitol, Didsbury, and the Victoria, Cambridge - the last two coming into the Union net in due course.

Frank Matthew was interested in transcribing well-known orchestral works for performance on the theatre organ and in particular he will be remembered for his arrangement of "In a Persian Market" by Albert Ketélby, adopted as recently as 1998 for a recording made by the American theatre organist Jonas Nordwall.

Frank Matthew remained at Slough and Windsor until the end of March 1934, being followed from 1 April by Rowland Tims FRCO, another pioneer with a cathedral training (Truro). He "toured the halls" with a large purpose-built straight orchestral organ with 5 manuals - a project later to be repeated by Reginald Foort with his Moller concert organ - before several years at the Capitol, Haymarket, London, playing to silent films on the big straight organ there and then interludes on the modern Compton cinema organ which replaced it in 1930. He remained at the Adelphi, Slough, and the Playhouse, Windsor, until leaving the company to join Paramount at their new cinema in Liverpool, broadcasting on a new type of 4-manual organ introduced by Compton for that chain. He was followed in October by Pierson Webber who was advertised as coming "from the Empire, Leicester Square" where he had been assistant to Sandy Macpherson; he did in fact hold that position for a while, but had also spent some time touring an important cinema circuit in Germany. He was to stay with Union for the remainder of the company's independent existence.

A small newly-built cinema was opened as the Regal, Bicester, in September 1934. The architect was Harold Scott of Birmingham, and there was seating for 504 persons on one floor.

David Bernhard announced the formation of a new company, Oxford & Berkshire Cinemas Ltd., which would acquire as a going concern ten cinemas in Oxford, Maidenhead, Banbury and Newbury currently operated by the Union Cinema Co. Ltd., the issue of shares being to provide funds for the construction of a new super cinema on the site occupied by the George Street Cinema, Oxford, and also to redeem bank mortgages and to enable the acquisition or construction of other cinemas as opportunities might arise. The new company was registered as a public company on 29 September 1934, with a nominal capital of £350,000 in the form of 150,000 7% cumulative participating preference shares of £1 each and 800,000 ordinary shares of 5s. each. The directors were to be David Bernhard, Frederick Bernhard and L.J.Clements. This was described as being the first of a series of new issues. The issue was very successful, being well over-subscribed.

At the Annual General Meeting of the Union Cinema Co. held on 17 October 1934, having announced satisfactory results, David Bernhard drew attention to an interesting aspect of the business not disclosed in the balance sheet: during the six years since it was formed, the company had been quietly building up an organisation capable of running a large circuit of cinemas. This process had involved a heavy charge on profits, but it would now be possible to move ahead with major expansion plans without any significant increase in overheads on this score. After the meeting Frederick Bernhard stated that the company was already in negotiation for several additional properties and that further finance would be needed.

The new cinema in Tunbridge Wells opened on 3 December 1934: called the Ritz, it was the first completely new cinema to be opened by Union Cinemas and was described in the local press as the finest and most luxurious cinema in the whole of Kent. Built on what was referred to as "the old Parham House site" at the corner of Mount Pleasant and Church Road, it formed the major part of a redevelopment which included fifteen shops ranged along the two frontages, with the cinema entrance on the corner itself. The scheme had been the brainchild of a businessman named J.O.Fairbrother and recognising the need for a modern cinema in the complex he had appointed N.D.Fitzgerald to direct this part of the project, thus explaining the Union Cinema Co.'s involvement. One of the leading specialists in cinema architecture, Robert Cromie FRIBA, was engaged to draw up the plans in a style which somewhat resembled that which he had previously adopted for another company, County Cinemas Ltd. The building work was entrusted to T.Bates & Sons who employed local labour for the work. An important feature of the exterior was an illuminated glass tower standing some 50ft high. The decorative scheme for the 1,600-seat auditorium was carried out in dull gold, sable and peach, with flame-coloured draperies. As yet the company had not settled on its own distinctive style, though this scheme suggested a progression towards it. The projection room was equipped with Kalee projectors and the Western Electric "Wide Range" sound system. The stage was fully equipped for the presentation of live performances. A Compton organ of 3 manuals and 7 pipe units was installed, with the addition of a "Solo Cello" attachment, this consisting of a real string "bowed" and played with mechanical fingering and amplified to reach the audience through a loudspeaker. The chambers were situated to the right of the proscenium, with the sound passing through the decorative grille on that side of the auditorium, and the console was as usual mounted on a lift in the centre of the orchestra pit. Perhaps surprisingly, it was fitted with a type of illuminated surround developed for ABC by Prides of Clapham, other companies being offered a variation known as the "Rainbow." The organ was described as having cost £7,000 - it is interesting that such round figures were often quoted on such occasions!

Adjoining the cinema was the Florida Restaurant, complete with dancing to the resident Ernest Loraine and his Band. For the Saturday night dinner-dances, evening dress was to be the rule!

The opening itself took place in the afternoon and was preceded by a special luncheon in the Florida Restaurant hosted by N.D.Fitzgerald. The guests included the Mayor and Mayoress, Mr and Mrs David Bernhard, Mr and Mrs Frederick Bernhard, Mr and Mrs L.J.Clements and a large number of local dignitaries. In addition, Robert Cromie was present, together with members of the Bates family, J.I.Taylor (Technical Director of the John Compton Organ Co.) and others involved with the building of the Ritz complex.

The special guest was Margaret Bannerman, the film actress who was starring with Matheson Lang in "The Defender" - one of the two feature films to be shown as part of the opening programme (the other being "Sing as we Go" with Gracie Fields). The opening ceremony itself of course took place on the stage and in the speeches much was made of the sheer Britishness of the occasion: the cinema and shopping complex itself built with British materials using British labour, the organ was British, too, the two feature films were both British, etc. The organ was played by Alex Taylor and was later described in the local press as "an organ of beautiful tone and immense power" - the latter perhaps a passing reference to Taylor's predilection for playing loudly! All in all, the arrangements for this opening really set the standard for future occasions, with little or no expense spared.

At the Ritz, Tunbridge Wells, live entertainment was initially confined to Sunday evening concerts, for example Elsie and Doris Waters, the delightful comedy act featuring "Gert and Daisy", on Sunday 23 December. The first weekday Cine-Variety show was not presented until 18 February 1935, with Nosmo King and three other acts. The name "Nosmo King" was a play on the words "No Smoking" which were to be found on signs in certain public areas in those days. However, the Sunday concerts continued to provide the more lavish fare: on 24 February Teddy Brown, the famous xylophonist, topped the bill, with Herschel Henlere, Bower & Rutherford and the Evelyn Hady Ladies Band; on 10 March it was the turn of Ronald Frankeau, cross-talk comedians Murray & Mooney, the Four Aces and Hal Swain and his Band.

On 6 December 1934 it was announced in the trade press that the authorised capital of the company was to be increased from £300,000 to £350,000 and that an Extraordinary General Meeting would be held on 28 December to consider and pass the necessary resolutions for the creation of 50,000 new shares of £1 each. The shares in the entire authorised capital would then be rearranged to give 200,000 7% cumulative participating preference shares and 150,000 ordinary shares of £1 each. This would include the conversion of some of the old ordinary shares already issued into 7% cumulative participating preference shares, thereby offering existing shareholders preferential rights of subscription. In addition, it was arranged that after the ordinary shares had received a similar dividend a further cumulative dividend of 3% would be payable on the preference shares ranking pari passu with a non-cumulative dividend of 3% on the ordinary shares, evidently an attractive package. In the event of liquidation, the preference shares would be repaid at par and after the ordinary shares had been repaid also the preference shareholders would receive 25% of any surplus available up to a maximum of 28s.6d. Otherwise, in accordance with normal practice, the preference shareholders would not enjoy voting powers so long as the 7% dividend was paid.

The commencement date for the revised scheme was to be 1 April 1935. It was stated that the increase in the authorised capital was needed for the expansion activities of the parent company and was not connected with any plans pending for the formation of further subsidiary companies.

Meanwhile, acquisitions continued to take place and an organ-equipped cinema taken over on 31 December was the Regal, Dewsbury. Dating from 1913 it was originally known as the Picture House, but many years later it was acquired by Lou Morris who carried out a scheme of modernisation as a 919-seater cinema in 1933. Despite this, the cinema remained a somewhat unprepossessing house. A small Compton organ of 3 manuals (one of them a coupler manual) and 5 pipe units with illuminated console of the ABC type was also installed. The cinema was reopened at Christmas 1933 as the Regal, the organist for the occasion being Anthony Zala.

From February to July 1935 the resident organist at the Regal, Dewsbury, was none other than Max Erard, the first to tour the country's variety theatres with a pipe organ. This he did as "Herr Max Erard" before World War I, the organ being a small 2-manual pipe organ built by Norman & Beard but made to appear larger than it actually was. Needless to say, soon after the outbreak of war the "Herr" was deleted from all publicity matter! Appearing with him was his wife, starring as "Zona Vevey", who had a pleasant soprano voice. Erard himself was described as a pale slim man with a Beethovenesque mop of hair and a florid style of playing; his real name was less exotic and in earlier days he had been organist of a non-conformist church in the North of England! After the war he accompanied silent films in Yorkshire cinemas and for a time he also took over a public house in which he had a pipe organ - another "first", perhaps?

After the departure of Max Erard, two Union organists made appearances at the Regal, Dewsbury. Alex Taylor was there for four weeks, commencing 2 September 1935, followed by the relative newcomer Jack Dowle for two weeks, commencing 30 September.

Jack Dowle had made his first appearance for Union Cinemas at the Ritz, Tunbridge Wells, on 22 July, continuing there until the end of August and then transferring to the Super, Gravesend week commencing 2 September before travelling North. Like so many others, he had started his career as a church organist and had held a number of appointments in the London area before deciding to seek more remunerative employment in the world of show business. His first engagement was as pianist in the orchestra at the Leicester Square Theatre. He later met Harold Ramsay, Musical Director of Bernstein Theatres Ltd, owners of the Granada cinema chain. Ramsay engaged him as his assistant and house organist at the flagship Granada, Tooting, in South London. Whilst there, Jack Dowle took part in important stage presentations devised by Harold Ramsay, notably "The Eight Piano Symphony" and the "Rhythm Symphony Orchestra" which I will refer to again in a later chapter. Moving on, he joined the growing team of organists employed by Union Cinemas. As we shall see, Ramsay himself would in due course be persuaded to take the position of Musical Director of the Company.

After his visit to Dewsbury, Jack Dowle returned to Tunbridge Wells on 14 October for a seven-week run. After that, a new resident arrived on the scene: "The Well-known Dewsbury Organist" Norman Gooder. He remained at the Regal for some time, but headed south to appear at the Super, Gravesend, for two weeks from 13 January 1936. In his absence a young 22-year-old organist arrived from the Lonsdale, Carlisle, to entertain the Dewsbury audiences: his name was Joseph Seal and he was presently to become one of the most celebrated members of the Union team.

Incidentally, it is worth noting that during Jack Dowle's absence from Tunbridge Wells, his place was taken by guest organist Reginald New, one of the country's great pioneer cinema organists. Between November 1929 and July 1933 he gave no less than four hundred and sixty-eight broadcasts from the Beaufort, Washwood Heath, Birmingham, before following Reginald Foort at the Regal, Kingston, for two years from August 1933 and giving well over another hundred broadcasts from there. Over the years he also broadcast several times from Cheltenham Town Hall on the fine concert organ installed there - these programmes normally included classical items but offered lighter fare as well, often turning straight organ stops to unorthodox use! He was a particularly fine musician who continued to entertain audiences for many years until his untimely death in 1958.

Another cinema acquired on 31 December 1934 was the Empire, Ashton-under-Lyne. This had originally been a theatre but later changed to cinema use and in 1933 underwent modernisation to plans of the architects Drury & Gomersall. Equipped as it was with a good stage and a suite of nine dressing rooms, and seating 1600 patrons, Union Cinemas recognised its potential for the presentation of Cine-Variety. The company had already embarked on this policy at Gravesend and Tunbridge Wells and intended to continue to implement it elsewhere in the future. However, there was no organ and the decision was therefore taken to rectify this by placing an order for a Compton standard model of 3 manuals (one a coupler manual) and 6 units with a "Rainbow" illuminated surround. With the idea of achieving maximum publicity in due course, this was kept very quiet. At the end of April 1935 a stage show was presented, with music supplied by a band; then on 11 May the local press advertisement carried the words "An army of workmen are at present preparing the Biggest Surprise of the Year in Ashton Theatre Entertainment" followed by "Remember: Monday next at 2.30 pm." On the Monday, 13 May, the illuminated console of the new organ duly rose from the pit to stage level, with Alex Taylor playing!

In addition to the work of preparing for the installation of the organ, a new cinema screen had been fitted which could be raised and lowered quickly and easily by means of counter-weighting, greatly facilitating presentation of the stage shows. It also transpired that the manager appointed to the "New Empire" to supervise the various improvements was none other than Captain Rifkin who had been in charge at the Super, Gravesend.

The policy of 50% films 50% variety took off in earnest from the week commencing 20 May, with Alex Taylor at the organ and accompanying the stage acts. Taylor actually stayed for the first fourteen weeks, after which he was replaced by Neville Meale who took over for ten weeks commencing 19 August, but by this time the stage shows had tended to become somewhat less frequent, occurring only for six weeks out of the ten. Meale returned to Gravesend week commencing 28 October, but then returned to the Empire where he was eventually followed by Pierson Webber from week commencing 9 December. These three organists continued to appear from time to time until April 1936, after which several others were to follow. One of these was "The Famous American Lady Organist, Elaine Bair" who was soon to be featured strongly throughout the circuit, including two BBC broadcasts in March 1937. I do not have many details, but believe it is possible that either Harold Ramsay or Alex Taylor may have known of her during their touring days in the United States and recommended that she join the Union team. Stage shows also continued, including a Christmas Pantomime starring Gertie Gitana and G.H.Elliott (known as "The Chocolate Coloured Coon"). In March the Ashton Operatic Society took the place over to present their annual amateur performance.

Another cinema acquired during this period was the Majestic, King's Lynn, an imposing 1928 house owned by one E.R.Adams: this purchase was made partly to obtain the services of Mr Adams as an administrator at Head Office and partly to attempt to achieve a monopoly in King's Lynn.

Two important appointments were announced in August. William Southan Morris was to be General Manager of the Union Cinema Co. Ltd. His contract was to run for five years. As previously mentioned, he had already been closely involved with the running of the company for some time. The other appointment was of J.H.Lundy, to be Director of Theatre Construction; previously he had acted as Theatre Controller. With the huge building programme planned by the company, this was clearly a major role within the organisation.

The next major opening took place on Saturday 5 October: the Ritz, Maidstone. This was in fact a reconstruction of the former Pavilion Picture House in Pudding Lane. The Pavilion itself had originally been a roller skating rink before being converted into a cinema. The architects employed for the reconstruction, Leslie Kemp & Tasker, made effective use of the existing building to bring it into line with modern requirements. Three glass doors gave access to the rather shallow entrance hall, the paybox being placed centrally with doors to the stalls on either side of it and stairs to the balcony situated on the extreme left and right. The predominant colour in this area was green. The auditorium was fitted with brown carpeting with semi-tub chairs supplied by the theatre furnishing company Pixtons, these having curved backs of exceptional depth for extra comfort. They were upholstered in a diamond-patterned brown. The side walls were also finished in brown to head height and then in rose with green motifs. The old balcony was retained, its front also finished in rose with vertical green bars. The proscenium was some 36ft wide and flanked by grilles in grey and gold. A Compton organ of 3 Manuals and 6 pipe units was installed and was unusual in being supplied with two consoles: a mobile one with "Rainbow" illuminated surround on the stage and one with wooden casing of standard pattern in a fixed position in the orchestra pit. It was also fitted with an early example of the patent Melotone unit, an electronic device capable of producing additional tones of a special character not otherwise obtainable. Perhaps not surprisingly, the publicity on this occasion declared that the organ had cost £10,000!

The opening ceremony was performed by the Mayor, accompanied by the Mayoress, and there was a guest appearance by Leonora Corbett, one of the stars appearing in the main feature film being shown: "Heart's Desire" with Richard Tauber. The film programme also included a newsreel and two new Walt Disney cartoons. On stage were Bobby Powell and his Band, while the organ interlude was presented by Alex Taylor and Pierson Webber featuring the two consoles.

Pierson Webber continued to appear weekly until the end of week commencing 2 December 1935, after which he went up to Ashton-under-Lyne. Alex Taylor then returned for one week and was followed by the "special engagement" of Lloyd Thomas from the Bernstein Theatres' Granada circuit who remained until the end of January 1936 when he moved to the Ritz, Tunbridge Wells, and then set out on a short tour of some of the other Union houses in the southern area. Neville Meale took over at Maidstone.

It is worthy of note that throughout the week following the opening of the Ritz, the nearby Granada, Maidstone, provided strong competition by featuring none other than Harold Ramsay himself, certainly one of the country's most popular organists, famous for his long series of broadcasts from the Granada, Tooting. The Maidstone Granada was equipped with an effective Christie organ of 3 manuals and 9 pipe units, making it a larger instrument than the Compton at the Ritz, notwithstanding the latter's two consoles! At the Ritz stage shows were of course included in the programme along with the organ interlude and by the end of the year several well-known artistes had appeared, including the celebrated comedians Max and Harry Nesbitt and "Hutch" - Leslie Hutchinson, a popular cabaret singer and frequent broadcaster who accompanied himself at the grand piano.

Also in October the company results were published for the year ending 31 March, showing a highly satisfactory situation with a net profit after taxation of £23,695 (which might not seem very much by today's standards but which was considered a goodly sum at the time). Ordinary shareholders were to receive a double dividend of 20% and a bonus issue of one new share for every twenty held. The directors drew attention to the fact that the value of the shares as shown in the balance sheet at par was substantially higher than that in terms of current stock market quotations. Herein might have lain one of the germs leading to the financial problems which were to afflict the company later on.

The good results produced a jump of 5s.9d. in the price of the ordinary shares to £3.12s.6d. and of 1s.3d. for the preference shares to £1.10s.0d. on the week. The Oxford & Berkshire shares also performed well, the ordinary rising 1s.6d. to 11s.6d. and the preference rising 2s.0d. to £1.14s.0d.

Negotiations for further important acquisitions were proceeding meanwhile, together with ambitious building plans for the future, and these will be described in the following chapter.

CHAPTER TWO

THE ACQUISITION TRAIL

During the first week of November 1935 it was announced that a further twenty-three cinemas had been acquired, including those in the Sidney Bacon circuit and those controlled by Walter Bentley in the Eastbourne, Hastings and St Leonards area of Sussex. The published list was as follows:

Majestic, Belfast	Electric Palace, Highgate
Strand, Belfast	Empire, Highgate
Regal, Bexley Heath	Capitol, Horsham
Victoria, Cambridge	Carfax, Horsham
City Picture House, Carlisle	Winter Gardens, Horsham
Lonsdale, Carlisle	Olympia, Newcastle
Public Hall, Carlisle	Elite, St Leonards
Regal, Cleethorpes	Regal, St Leonards
Princess, Crayford	Rivoli, Southend
Luxor, Eastbourne	Kosmos, Tunbridge Wells
Picture House, Erith	Opera House, Tunbridge Wells
Cinema de Luxe, Hastings	

This list includes some new purpose-built houses with modern equipment and furnishings; others were vintage halls of varying standards. Of the two Belfast cinemas, another month was to pass before the Strand opened its doors and the Majestic was not ready until the following May. The Regal, Cleethorpes, was evidently a project for the future: the Ritz, Cleethorpes, not opening until July 1937. The Regal, Bexley Heath, had been opened as recently as 3 September 1934 and was equipped with a

Compton organ of 3 manuals and 8 units plus Solo Cello attachment, opened by H.Robinson Cleaver ARCO who had transferred from the Lonsdale, Carlisle, where he had been resident for the previous three years and before that at the Piccadilly, Manchester, for over four years. Cleaver was featured regularly at Bexley Heath throughout 1935 and commenced broadcasting from there on 7 January 1936, his signature tune "An Earful of Music" guaranteeing enjoyable listening. The Lonsdale, Carlisle, possessed a Christie organ of 2 manuals and 9 units, on which Cleaver's successor Joseph Seal had commenced broadcasting on 9 October 1935; his first appointment as a cinema organist had been at the Regal, Altrincham, where he was resident for one year before moving to Carlisle. It was there that he adopted as his signature tune the Cumberland folksong "D'ye ken John Peel." Both these organists were to enjoy distinguished careers in their chosen field. The Rivoli, Southend, had a Christie organ of 2 manuals and 8 units divided to either side of the auditorium and the Victoria, Cambridge, had another divided Christie, this time of 3 manuals and 7 units. Small Compton organs of 3 manuals and 6 units were to be found at the Regal, St Leonards, opened 8 August 1932, and the Luxor, Eastbourne, opened 3 April 1933, the third manual in each case being a coupler manual. The three cinemas in Horsham were acquired from Blue Flash Cinemas, a company formed by a group of officers formerly with the Royal Sussex Regiment, one of the objects being to provide employment for local men who had served with that regiment.

Frederick Bernhard went on to state that negotiations were well advanced for further acquisitions to be made and that another share issue would be required to provide additional finance. As it was, all these developments involved a total purchase price of some £3,000,000, largely financed out of the company's own resources, partly by cash and partly by the security of existing freehold properties already owned outright.

The same November press release also referred to ambitious plans for new construction. A large Ritz cinema was being built in Belfast and sites had been acquired for new cinemas in the following towns:

Banbury	Dunstable	Luton
Bath	Hereford	Macclesfield
Chatham	Horsham	Maidenhead
Cleethorpes	Huddersfield	Oldham
Darlington	Hyde	Penzance
Dukinfield	Ipswich	Tonbridge
		West Hartlepool

As we shall see, a considerable number of these projects came to fruition, but not all of them. Some appeared to be initiated by others, with the Union Cinema Co. taking over at some stage and applying the "Union" look to their completion and eventual opening. One such was the Strand, East Belfast, in which the subsidiary company was S.&U.Cinemas (Strand & Union?). The opening was performed by the Lord Mayor of Belfast on 9 December in the presence of the architect, J.M'Bride Neil, and J.H.Lundy and others representing Union. As with other openings, the scenes outside and in the vestibule were filmed for showing on the screen later. This cinema was described in the press as being the company's first in Northern Ireland.

The next share issue involved the flotation of National Provincial Cinemas Ltd in December. The authorised capital was to be £750,000 and the issue was to comprise 325,000 6% cumulative participating preference shares of £1 each to be offered at 22s. per share and 1,000,000 ordinary shares of 5s. each. The Directors were to be: David Bernhard (Chairman), Charles Frederick Bernhard (Managing director), William Southan Morris (General Manager) and Lawrence Joseph Clements. The company would acquire as going concerns the following 13 cinemas:

Regal, Bexley Heath	Empire, Highgate
City Picture House, Carlisle	Capitol, Horsham
Lonsdale, Carlisle	Carfax, Horsham
Public Hall, Carlisle	Winter Garden, Horsham
Princess, Crayford	Olympia, Newcastle
Picture House, Erith	Rivoli, Southend
Electric Palace, Highgate	

In addition, the company would own the whole of the issued share capital of Southan Morris Circuit Ltd. together with certain shares in Windsor Playhouse Ltd. and Uxbridge Entertainments Ltd. which owned or controlled through subsidiaries the following:

Palace, Dunstable	Regal, Windsor
Empire, Luton	Playhouse, Windsor
Picturedrome, Luton	Royalty, Windsor
Plaza, Luton	New Empire, Wolverton
Adelphi, Slough	Marlborough, Yiewsley
Regal, Uxbridge	

The prospectus also mentioned that Southan Morris Circuit Ltd. owned a substantial interest in the company operating the Ritz, Central Playhouse and Palace cinemas in Maidstone. The cinemas listed above were something of a mixed bag, but of particular interest was the Regal, Uxbridge, which had been opened on 26 December 1931 by an important figure in the cinema world, A.E.Abrahams. The architect had been E. Norman Bailey and the cinema was a good example of the stadium type of layout, with all of the 1610 seats arranged on one floor. There was a small Compton organ of 2 manuals and 6 units, the console being in a fixed position in the pit. There was no illuminated surround, but the design of the casework somewhat resembled that of the Wurlitzer "French" type, having side pillars with curved cappings - Comptons built a number of these at about that time.

My researches indicate that the organ had not been featured very much prior to the Southan Morris acquisition - leading of course to Union involvement. Prior to this, there had been stage shows featuring one act only rather than the more usual three or four, but with no mention of organ accompaniment. Under the new management, the advertisement block for the Regal was moved from the bottom to the top of the entertainments page in the local newspaper. For the week commencing 7 October it included the announcement "First time in Uxbridge! 50% Variety 50% Films" - but with still no mention of the organ. These more ambitious stage shows were presented each week until the week commencing 4 November when special guest organist Gordon Spicer appeared instead. The following week Alex Taylor appeared for the first time, with the billing "Special engagement of the world-famous exponent of the unit organ, in a new and novel organ presentation." By popular demand he was retained for a second week and was followed by another guest, Stanley Todd and then Jack Dowle, for one week each. After that, Neville Meale arrived week commencing 9 December for a five week run.

At the end of 1935 Frederick Bernhard spelled out Union Cinemas' policy: the aim was to secure control of all of the cinemas in a given town and this had already been achieved in a number of places. Where this could not be done, the aim was certainly to control the best cinema in the town. He had previously stated that the company would seek to build a modern cinema in every town where one did not already exist, taking the name Ritz whenever possible, with Regal as second choice. On the face of it, this policy did not seem unreasonably ambitious. However, there were to be many pitfalls and problems along the way: planning permissions were not always readily forthcoming, strong opposition was often mounted by existing exhibitors and there was also intense competition at times from other companies, particularly Odeon Theatres whom the Bernhards considered presented the most serious threat to their building plans. In addition to new building projects already listed, the following were stated to be in various stages of planning:

Blackpool	Leek	Rotherham
Burnley	Lincoln	Sheffield
Eastbourne	Middlesbrough	Stafford
Enfield	Newport	Stretford
Gravesend	Rawtenstall	Surbiton
Halifax	Ripon	Swansea
Herne Bay	Rochdale	Worksop

Another six were planned for Northern Ireland:

Ballymena	Larne	Londonderry
Coleraine	Lisburn	Lurgan

References will be made to several of these in the chapters which follow. Some schemes progressed further than others, while some in fact made no real progress at all.

Meanwhile, negotiations continued apace for further acquisitions and at the beginning of January 1936 a press release announced that deals had been made involving the A.H.Reed circuit, Mancunian Cinemas Ltd., Aberdeen Picture Palace Ltd., Caledonian Theatres Ltd., Harris Brothers of Falmouth, A.G.Iggledon, Great Yarmouth Theatre Properties Ltd. and the Majestic (Darlington) Ltd. The cinemas were listed as follows:

Regal, Kingston	Astoria, Aberdeen
Regal, Beckenham	Belmont, Aberdeen
Regal, Altrincham	Capitol, Aberdeen
Lido, Burnage	City, Aberdeen
Riviera, Cheetham Hill	Globe, Aberdeen
Capitol, Didsbury	King's, Aberdeen
Broadway, Eccles	Majestic, Aberdeen
Kingsway, Levenshulme	Playhouse, Aberdeen
Pyramid, Sale	Star, Aberdeen
Central, Folkestone	Casino, Herne Bay
Playhouse, Folkestone	Red Lantern, Herne Bay
Pleasure Gardens, Folkestone	Grand, Falmouth

Plaza, Catford	St.George's Hall, Falmouth
Palace, Eltham	Whitehall, Rotherham
Regal, Sidcup	Majestic, Darlington
Alma, Luton	Regal, Great Yarmouth

In making this announcement it could be argued that to a certain extent the company was "jumping the gun." Whilst negotiations may indeed have reached an advanced stage, in the event not all of these deals were successfully concluded. Most importantly, those intended to achieve control of most, if not all, of the cinemas in Aberdeen failed to go through, with the company withdrawing from the talks. At the end of January it was being claimed that a controlling interest had been obtained in the Belmont and Majestic cinemas, owned by Caledonian Theatres Ltd., and of the Astoria, owned by Aberdeen Astoria Ltd., but had so far not succeeded in acquiring holdings in Aberdeen Picture Palaces Ltd. which owned six important cinemas in the city. A week later it was reported that the company was "acquiring" the controlling interest in Caledonian and Astoria and that the plans provided for the setting up of a special holding company with Frederick Bernhard and Bert Darley, the managing director of Astoria, as joint managing directors. The following week came the announcement that the whole scheme had been dropped and that Union had withdrawn "for various reasons."

The Capitol, Aberdeen, had a Compton organ of 3 manuals and 8 units which at the time was being broadcast regularly by Harold Coombs: a few years later he would be appointed Chief Organist for Associated British Cinemas, based at the Regal, Kingston! The Astoria, too, had a Compton organ.

With regard to Mancunian Cinemas Ltd., most of the cinemas concerned were acquired, but not the Pyramid, Sale, or the Lido, Burnage. The Riviera, Cheetham Hill, was held for only a short time. However, good representation was achieved in the Greater Manchester area, including some really important cinemas.

The Pyramid, Sale, would have been a remarkable addition to the circuit: as implied by its name, its architectural design gave an impression of "Ancient Egypt", carried through from the exterior facade into the vestibule and auditorium and even the casework of the organ console on the stage! The organ was a Christie of 3 manuals and 7 units and had a second console (with plain casework) in the pit. It was being broadcast regularly by Reginald Liversidge who presumably would have joined the Union team of organists if the deal had gone through. However, it was not to be.

Negotiations for the Majestic, Darlington, were still continuing right through into March, the intention being to transfer ownership to National Provincial Cinemas Ltd., but eventually this deal failed also.

As acquisitions proceeded over a period of time, an increasing number of the more recently-built "super cinemas" came into the net as distinct from older halls of the "flea pit" variety, virtually all of them having been built and opened since the Union Cinema Co. first came into being.

The Regal, Kingston, was chosen to be the new flagship of the greatly enlarged circuit. This splendid cinema had already been made famous by the many broadcasts by organists Reginald Foort, Reginald New and Rex O'Grady on the unique Wurlitzer organ - a 3-manual "special" originally built for the residence of a Chicago millionaire and containing some refined and distinctive voicing. For its installation at Kingston it was somewhat enlarged to include 12 pipe units and a grand piano attachment. The organ chambers were on the roof of the building, with the swell shutters facing towards the stage. The sounds of the instrument travelled down a curved tone-chute to reach the auditorium through concealed openings in the top of the proscenium. The Regal had originally opened its doors on 15 February 1932. Designed by the architect Robert Cromie, the magnificent auditorium had seating for 2,433 patrons, a fully equipped stage with fly tower and a suite of dressing rooms for live entertainment, plus a café-restaurant situated above the foyer.

Another cinema with an interesting history was the Capitol, Didsbury. This had first opened on 21 February 1931 but had been gutted by fire on 25 April 1932, leaving only the front of the building and the outer walls standing. Its success had been such as to guarantee not only prompt rebuilding but the addition of a number of novel new features. The new cinema was opened on 16 August 1933 and was equipped with a remarkable new lighting system for the proscenium and auditorium which could be controlled from the organ console, in theory enabling the organist to obtain lighting effects to suit the type of music he happened to be playing. The original organ had been a Christie of 3 manuals and 8 units, opened by Frank Matthew, and by popular demand this was replaced by another Christie, this time enlarged to 4 manuals and 10 units plus a "phantom" grand piano on the stage. It was opened by Edward O'Henry who became the resident organist and soon afterwards began regular broadcasts. The stage itself was deepened and fitted with a revolve. Following its acquisition by Union, the Capitol was soon chosen to be the No. 1 house in the North and it was the first provincial cinema to be visited by Harold Ramsay after his appointment as Musical Director in 1936. In due course it would also become the base for organist Cecil Chadwick and the organ would be broadcast frequently by him and occasionally by others.

Another cinema with a Christie organ was the Broadway, Eccles, this being of 3 Manuals and 7 units, opened on 29 July 1932 by Thomas Dando, whilst the Kingsway, Levenshulme, had an organ of 3 manuals and 10 units built by the local Manchester firm of Jardine, opened on 15 March 1929 by the well-known Manchester organist and composer Norman Cocker.

The Regal, Beckenham, had a Wurlitzer organ of 2 manuals and 8 units, and some of the other cinemas listed above had Compton organs of varying sizes. One of these was the Alma, Luton, where the organ had been installed originally in 1930 with 2 manuals and 6 units; in 1934 a third (coupler) manual was added, together with an illuminated console surround.

Apart from the fine new cinemas built to modern standards, several of the older ones were inspected and evaluated for reconstruction and refurbishment, just as had happened at the Super, Gravesend, and remained company policy.

Having dealt with the acquisitions, the same press release in early January 1936 went on to announce that a contract had been signed with Arthur Segal for the construction of some forty new cinemas to be erected in various parts of the country. A feature of these would be the provision of facilities for live entertainment on stage in addition to the film shows, much on the lines introduced by Segal when he built the large Astorias in the London area during the period 1929-31. The first list to be published was as follows:

Ritz, Aldershot	Ritz, Hastings
Ritz, Barnsley	Ritz, Herne Bay
Ritz, Bexhill	Ritz , Horsham
Ritz, Chatham	Ritz, Ipswich
Ritz , Cleethorpes	Ritz , Richmond
Regal, Cowley (Oxford)	Ritz , Scunthorpe
Ritz, Eastbourne	Ritz , Woking

The name "Regal" was chosen for the cinema at Cowley as the new cinema in George Street, Oxford, now well on the way to completion, was designated "Ritz." It will be noted that some of the locations listed above had already been announced, together with certain others, the previous November. Work on one of the latter, the new cinema at Huddersfield, was in fact already well advanced. The plans for the cinemas on the latest list were to be drawn up by two of the most distinguished firms of architects, Robert Cromie and Verity & Beverley.

Problems could and did arise: for example, the application to build at Aldershot was turned down by the Borough Council in mid-February, supposedly on the grounds that the elevation of the building as planned was unsatisfactory. However, it seemed more likely that there were worries that another cinema in the town might result in over-seating. The company evidently continued its lobbying, as in mid-March it was announced that a revised elevation had been approved, but now the Works Committee wanted the scheme to be turned down because of certain bye-laws connected with the proposed site. These further objections were evidently overcome, as by the end of April the trade press announced that the new cinema would be built on the site next door to the Empire cinema (owned by County Cinemas Ltd.).

As we shall see, for a wide variety of reasons not all of the cinemas planned by Union were actually built. For example, having failed to obtain control of the Majestic, Darlington, the company proposed to build another cinema there and negotiations were set in motion to acquire a key site in the town. However, objectors won the day on the grounds that there were already six existing cinemas within 300 yards of the proposed site and the opening of a seventh would result in saturation. Nothing more was done.

CHAPTER THREE

TWIN DEBUT - WURLITZER AND HAROLD RAMSAY

As mentioned earlier, Lloyd Thomas from the Bernstein Theatres' Granada circuit undertook a "special engagement" at the Ritz, Maidstone, starting week commencing 16 December 1935, remaining there until the end of January before setting out on a short tour of a number of Union cinemas in the southern area, including Tunbridge Wells, Eastbourne, St. Leonards, Slough and Uxbridge. It is interesting to note that Reginald Dixon, the famous organist of the tower Ballroom, Blackpool, who used to tour the Granada circuit in the winter months every year during the pre-war period, was booked to appear at the Regal, Bexley Heath, week commencing 27 January 1936. As if this was not enough, he was followed there the next week by the legendary Reginald Foort!

The first major opening in 1936 took place on 10 February: the Ritz, Huddersfield. There had been much controversy over the decision to erect a cinema on the site of the famous old Cloth Hall, but the Corporation seemed satisfied with the way in which the architect Robert Cromie had taken account of their wishes and recommendations in the matter of the building's design. With an auditorium seating 2,027 patrons, large stage, organ and Café-ballroom, the requirements of the company were fully met.

W. Southan Morris was responsible for the Opening Ceremony and from contemporary accounts this was a huge success. A trumpet fanfare opened the proceedings. On the stage the Mayor, accompanied by the Mayoress, made a short speech and declared the cinema open.

The actress Sally Gray and the comedy actor Sydney Howard were also present as special guests and both contributed speeches. Others present included David Bernhard, chairman of the Union Cinema Co.

The feature film was "First a Girl" and other items included a Silly Symphony and the Gaumont-British News. The stage show was presented by Billy Cotton and his Band, but the hit of the evening was undoubtedly Harold Ramsay at the Wurlitzer organ. "His initial appearance evoked a storm of applause, which became positively tumultuous at the conclusion of his Turn" - thus reported the local press! As I have already mentioned, Ramsay was at that time Musical Director of Bernstein Theatres Ltd., proprietors of the Granada circuit, and had been specially engaged for the opening at Huddersfield. He was one of the most popular cinema organists of the day and with his charismatic personality and showmanship he enjoyed outstanding success wherever he appeared. He was particularly well-known for his signature tune, the slow nostalgic theme from George Gershwin's "Rhapsody in Blue", which he had originally been given permission to use by Gershwin himself, and when he was playing an organ which had an illuminated console surround the lights would normally be held on Blue.

As to the organ itself, this installation was of special interest. The specification of the instrument was very similar to that of the Granada, Bedford, opened in December 1934. With the opening of a London factory the previous year to cut costs and afford greater flexibility, this was the first example of taking a standard Wurlitzer Model 190 of 2 manuals and 8 units and adding a coupler manual (as pioneered a few years earlier by the British organ-builder Compton) to give the appearance of a larger and more impressive instrument. Evidently it caught the attention of Union Cinemas, as having previously ordered only Compton organs for their new cinemas, they were now inspired not only to order a Wurlitzer organ for the first time but also to engage Ramsay to play it for the opening. The other important feature was the treatment of the console: the casework was painted gold, with a new type of music desk bearing the name "Wurlitzer" in raised letters in a fan-shaped arrangement, together with an illuminated surround and bench of the "Rainbow" style manufactured by F.H.Pride & Co. of Clapham. I believe this may have been the only Wurlitzer organ to be supplied with an illuminated bench (or "hot seat" as some organists described it!). In due course it was replaced by what was known as a Howard seat, consisting of a small upholstered swivel seat mounted on a single pillar which afforded audiences a clear view of the pedals, toe pistons and so on - not to mention the pedal technique of the organist - and so adding to the general impression of "mightiness". This type of seat became standard for most subsequent Union installations. The new style music desk became standard for the Union Wurlitzers to follow and was also adopted with minor variations by other companies.

Harold Ramsay remained at Huddersfield for the whole of the opening week and was then followed by another distinguished guest organist, Reginald Dixon. Thereafter, several members of the Union team appeared at the Ritz, including Alex Taylor, Neville Meale, Pierson Webber, Robinson Cleaver and Joseph Seal. Harold Ramsay returned for week commencing 8 June, by which time he was actually employed by the company.

There had been an opening of a relatively small cinema. the Ritz, Maidenhead, by the Mayor on 20 January but of course this had attracted much less publicity than the more ambitious project which followed a fortnight later in Huddersfield. It was newly built on the site of the old Picture Theatre, Maidenhead's first cinema, just opposite the Rialto. Seating fewer than 1,000 patrons, the Ritz auditorium was long in relation to its width and had no balcony. The colour scheme was green and orange, with black doors with stainless steel fittings. The compact projection room was equipped with two Simplex projectors and Western Electric sound system.

In January P. Allender Fryer was appointed to the Alma, Luton, and after a few weeks began to tour the circuit, remaining with Union for one year. Occasionally billed as Allen Fryer, he was another classically-trained organist who later switched to the cinema organ and who first broadcast in 1929. He had been a student of the great Dr.G.D.Cunningham, organist to the City of Birmingham and previously of Alexandra Palace.

February saw the arrival of Paul Gomez and his partner Miss Barrie Moore: together they presented what was billed as "A Novel Musical Divertissement." Gomez was a particularly interesting musician, having trained originally as a violinist and worked professionally with the orchestra of the Carl Rosa Opera Company. He had also toured with an orchestra conducted by the great English composer Elgar and had appeared at State functions at Buckingham Palace. In America he studied the organ and worked in a number of New York cinemas in the days of silent films. Back in this country he continued in the field of entertainment, latterly with Bernstein Theatres including Harold

Ramsay's "Rhythm Symphony" and "The Granada Serenaders" - a small group of instrumentalists and singers - before commencing his partnership with Barrie Moore. Together, they toured the Granada circuit and then switched to Union Cinemas.

In March another guest organist was Jack Courtnay, elder brother of Alex Taylor and arguably the very first exponent of the Wurlitzer in this country. He toured the circuit rather more extensively and remained on the scene longer than Lloyd Thomas.

Towards the end of March it was announced that John Jarrett, Manager of the Gravesend group of cinemas (Super, Plaza, Majestic and Regal) had been appointed circuit manager for the 22 Union Cinemas located in the south-east. Earlier in his career he had been manager of the Astoria, Old Kent Road, London, when it opened on 10 February 1930.

At the beginning of April the ordinary shares of the Union Cinema Co. stood at £8.15s.0d. and the preference at £1.10s.0d.; the National Provincial ordinary at 15s.6d. and the preference at £1.5s.3d.; and the Oxford and Berkshire shares remained steady, ex-dividend. By the end of the third week of April, Union Cinemas ordinary had risen to £10.10s.0d., so clearly the enterprise of these associated companies was by now attracting considerable attention from investors: satisfactory dividends were being paid and plans for the future appeared to indicate that things were moving into "top gear."

An important change took place in Gravesend: the success of the Super had attracted audiences away from other cinemas in the town and the owners of one of these, the Majestic, a larger hall seating 1,838 patrons and originally opened in 1931, took the decision to compete by installing a Compton organ of 3 manuals and 7 units with a "phantom" grand piano on the stage and an illuminated console mounted on a turntable lift. This was opened by Reginald New on 25 February. At the same time some refurbishment was undertaken, including new curtains and lighting.

At the Super, Alex Taylor and Neville Meale continued to appear at the organ, with occasional appearances by other members of the Union team, but it became clear that the competition now being offered by the Majestic was altogether too strong. In due course it was decided that the best course of action would be for Union Cinemas to take over the Majestic and downgrade the Super. I am not clear as to how long the negotiations leading to the eventual acquisition of the Majestic actually took, but I believe control finally passed to Union in April 1936. The last solo organ interludes at the Super were given by Alex Taylor week commencing 2 March, after which no further interludes were advertised at either the Super or the Majestic until week commencing 10 August when Harold Ramsay appeared at the Majestic. In due course the small Compton organ at the Super was removed for use elsewhere.

Another addition to the circuit was the Rota, Denton (Greater Manchester) which was acquired from Jackson & Newport (Lancashire) Ltd., effective from 4 April.

The opening of the Ritz, Oxford, took place on 20 April and marked the next major achievement in the company's building programme. As usual, the opening ceremony was performed by the Mayor, accompanied by the Mayoress, in the presence of the local Member of Parliament and other dignitaries, making it an important occasion in the city. Gaumont-British cameramen were present to film the proceedings, to be shown on the screen during the week.

The plans for the Ritz had been drawn up by Robert Cromie and provided for the main entrances and lobby to face a new road constructed at right-angles to George Street, with the left hand side of the building running along George Street itself. Evidently this arrangement was adopted in order to maximise the seating capacity of the auditorium, having regard to the limitations of the site, and seats were actually provided for 1,654 patrons. Mahogany was used for the doors and the interior colour scheme was carried out in beige, pink and gold treated to give a mottled effect. The proscenium was framed by a lighting cove and incorporated a grille for the organ chambers situated overhead. The stage was of course fully equipped for the presentation of live entertainment, in line with company policy. The projection room was fitted with Kalee projectors and Western Electric sound system. Above the entrance foyer was the café, decorated with gold ornamentation and mirrored walls, together with a large window overlooking the new road and featuring a pleasant sand-blasted design. In general it could be fairly said of the Ritz, Oxford, that it marked the commencement of the true "Union" style of cinema.

The organ was a Compton of 3 manuals and 6 pipe units, plus the patent Melotone electronic unit and a "phantom" grand piano on the stage. The console was mounted on a lift in the centre of the orchestra pit and was fitted with a "Rainbow" illuminated surround. Alex Taylor played for the opening and there was a spectacular stage show which included Macari and his Dutch Accordion Serenaders, dancing by the Ten Gordon Ray Girls, the remarkable balancing act of The Seven Graysons and the Royal Command cartoonist Van Dock. Alex Taylor remained for the first four weeks, followed by Robinson Cleaver and Pierson Webber.

Whether or not the Union management already had Harold Ramsay in mind for the position of Musical Director before his enormously successful appearance at the opening of the Ritz, Huddersfield, there can be little doubt that this event counted heavily in reaching the decision to offer him the appointment ("We *must* have him!" etc.). Certainly his achievements at Bernstein Theatres would not have gone unnoticed. As Ramsay himself related many years later, the Bernsteins were approached with a view to releasing him and in due course this was agreed.

Ramsay had been born in Norfolk but emigrated to Canada with his parents while still a youngster. Living in Calgary, Alberta, his musical talents were quickly recognised and on leaving high school he studied at the Conservatory of Music at Mount Royal College in that town, later joining the teaching staff for a time. He also held appointments as church organist in the area when still in his teens. After gaining his Licentiate in Music from McGill University in 1921 he travelled to New York and continued classical organ studies with the legendary Lynwood Farnum. Then in 1923 he began a three-year engagement at the Rivoli Theatre, New York City, as organist and assistant conductor of the large orchestra. During this period he claimed to have been the first organist to broadcast and the first to introduce community singing by the audience. Then from 1926 to 1932 he was employed by Paramount Theatres and toured throughout the United States, often flying his own aircraft to distant venues. Harold Ramsay's return to England came about as the result of the Bernstein brothers making an approach to Paramount to see if they would send over one of their organists, things "American" at that time being considered very trendy and up-to-date. He was the obvious choice as being Canadian he could claim British citizenship. His initial appearance was very successful and he was offered a permanent position, so after returning briefly to America to settle his affairs over there he came back and took up his duties at the company's flagship cinema, the Granada, Tooting, making his first broadcast from there on 29 December 1932. Apart from his musical skills he was a remarkable communicator with his audiences and quickly became an immensely popular artiste.

Harold Ramsay rapidly made a name for himself in this country, both by touring the Granada circuit and by broadcasting and making records on a regular basis. As Musical Director he was responsible for building up a team of fine organists for the steadily-growing chain of cinemas, some of them also broadcasting and recording. He supervised the enlargement of some of the existing organs - including the Wurlitzer at Tooting - and eventually developed specifications for new instruments for cinemas under construction, such as the Wurlitzer for the Granada, Bedford, on which the one for the Ritz, Huddersfield, was to be closely modelled. He designed a much larger Wurlitzer for what was to be the Granada, Manchester: with 4 manuals and 16 units it was basically an enlarged version of the organ at Tooting, but finally built with two of the units and two additional 16ft octaves of pipes deleted from the scheme, leaving the pipework almost identical to that at Tooting. However, the cinema itself was sold by Granada to the Gaumont-British Picture Corporation shortly before completion and it opened as the Gaumont on 21 October 1935. Today, this organ is still in existence and now forms part of the Granada Studios Tour in Manchester - thanks to the astonishing and heroic efforts of the Lancastrian Theatre Organ Trust. The original console, together with windchests and other important components, were lost in a fire while in storage and had to be replaced, but fortunately all of the pipework survived as it had been stored elsewhere. Harold Ramsay would in due course design another 16-unit Wurlitzer for the proposed new Union Cinemas flagship to be built in Richmond, but sadly the order for this instrument was cancelled. I believe it is more than likely that it would have been very similar to the one originally proposed for Manchester.

Harold Ramsay also devised some impressive musical stage presentations. One of these was "The Eight Piano Symphony" comprising a group of eight white grand pianos on which special arrangements of popular numbers were played by a team of performers headed by Clive Richardson and Tony Lowry. These two talented pianists were later to form their own act - "Four Hands in Harmony" - with which they toured extensively and gave over five hundred broadcasts, at the same time pursuing their own highly successful independent careers in the music business. A year later, in 1934, at the suggestion of the Director of the BBC Variety Department, Harold Ramsay produced the "Rhythm Symphony Orchestra" which gave a number of broadcasts and went out on a tour of the country, Ramsay conducting and also playing organ solos whenever the venue had a suitable organ available.

In addition, Harold Ramsay found fame as a composer of popular music, covering quite a wide field but specialising in ballads. One of these, "Her Name is Mary", became something of a "standard" and indeed I have heard it broadcast again while writing this book.

All in all, Harold Ramsay's work at Bernstein Theatres provided the perfect blueprint for the role he was invited to perform for Union Cinemas. A substantial increase in salary was offered and during April his appointment was announced. He gave his last broadcasts from Tooting and travelled north for the opening of the Plaza, Mansfield, a Bernstein house though not named Granada, on 20 April, the organ being an improved version of the 3-manual 8-unit Wurlitzers supplied to the Granada, Bedford, and the Ritz, Huddersfield. He remained at Mansfield for a second week and then proceeded directly to the Regal, Kingston, to take up his duties with Union Cinemas on 4 May, presenting a programme entitled "Audiences I have played for." Prior to his arrival, the Kingston Wurlitzer had been overhauled and cleaned and the console remodelled on the lines of the one at Huddersfield: the casework was repainted in gold, complete with the new type of music desk, and an illuminated surround was fitted. Rather curiously, the latter was not of the usual "Rainbow" style but of the slightly different type designed for Associated British Cinemas, with three graduated sections having curved fronts to either side and a flat-topped section across the top at the rear. As mentioned earlier, the organs at the Regal, Dewsbury, and the Ritz, Tunbridge Wells, were also fitted with this type of surround. I have not been able to discover why these exceptions should have occurred; perhaps they were the only surrounds readily available from stock at the time they were required. A new lift was installed at Kingston to accommodate the enlarged console layout, though still retaining the short travel with which in the "down" position the upper portion of the console was still visible to the audience. The original wooden bench was retained.

Harold Ramsay stayed at Kingston for the whole of May, after which he went up to the Capitol, Didsbury, for week commencing 1 June. Whilst there he took the opportunity to visit the other organ-equipped Union houses in the Greater Manchester area to inspect and try out the organs. One of these was the Regal, Altrincham, which had a Compton 3-manual 10-unit organ with an unusual disposition of the stopkeys and a divided top manual whereby different combinations of stops could be set up simultaneously for the bass and treble sections. These arrangements had been specified by the original organist, Norman Cocker. Ramsay decided that the entire layout should be rearranged in conventional order, partly to assist visiting organists on tour and partly because there was already a movement towards standardisation of console layouts on all newly-built cinema organs in this country, irrespective of builder and even including all new Wurlitzers imported from America. The following week, commencing 8 June, Harold Ramsay made a return visit to the Ritz, Huddersfield, but he was only able to appear from the Monday to the Friday, as on the Saturday he had to dash down to Horsham in Sussex for the opening of the Ritz in that town. The following week he would make his first appearance at the Ritz, Oxford.

On joining Union it quickly became clear that Harold Ramsay was to redouble his efforts in all respects. Apart from personal appearances around the circuit, he became heavily involved in design work for the new Wurlitzer and Compton organs that would be ordered for the new cinemas in the building programme, along with the recruitment of the additional organists needed to play them. The latter would be chosen not only for good playing skills plus the ability to accompany variety acts performing on stage but also to provide a mix of personalities who would project their individual brands of showmanship as they toured the circuit. It was almost certainly because of these preoccupations that he did not recommence his regular BBC broadcasts until August. When these did begin again they nearly always included a medley of popular songs of the day, with the audience joining in to sing a couple of them. His recording contract with Parlophone continued and in due course a total of eleven records were issued, all made at Kingston. One of them was devoted entirely to community singing by the audience, led by Ramsay at the organ. The cowboy song "Home on the Range" became a firm favourite at Kingston and was repeated on many occasions.

It should be remembered that prior to Harold Ramsay's arrival on the scene, Alex Taylor had held the position of Musical Director since August 1934 and so in the absence of any specific information on the subject I am inclined to assume that an accommodation must have been made which was acceptable to him. Alex Taylor had been appearing at the openings of new cinemas added to the circuit and in fact he continued to do so on several more occasions - indeed he was to remain with the company after Ramsay's departure later on. It would appear, therefore, that he continued to enjoy a certain seniority throughout the heyday of the company.

On 25 May the second new cinema in Northern Ireland, the Majestic, was opened in the Lisburn Road, Belfast, by one of the local councillors in the presence of the Lord Mayor. As with the Strand, this was operated by S.&U. Cinemas and once again J.M'Bride Neill was the architect. Seating was provided for 1,369 patrons. The facade was dressed throughout with faience and this, together with the interior decoration, was to give the building a decidedly "non-Union" appearance. It was said later that it closely resembled that of the Odeon, Surbiton - almost a carbon copy, in fact!

Following the appointment of Harold Ramsay as Musical Director, the first new organist to join the team was Gordon Banner who made his first appearance at the Ritz, Maidstone, week commencing 1 June. Born in Australia, he came to this country when he was sixteen years of age. Later, after gaining a Bachelor of Arts Degree at Oxford, he moved to Canada where, among other exploits, he became a "star" dirt-track rider and for a time he was billed as "The World Champion Wall of Death Rider." This involved riding a motor-cycle at high speed round a sort of inverted cylinder and climbing steadily towards the top, centrifugal force alone preventing him from falling. The whole spectacular feat was performed to the acclamation of the paying onlookers! Later still, Gordon Banner moved to the United States where his musical prowess came to prominence when he played with the Paul Whiteman Orchestra and for a while acted as assistant to the great cinema organist Jesse Crawford. On joining Union Cinemas he was billed as "The Ace Australian Organist."

One week later, on 8 June, Phil Park made his debut at the Regal, Kingston. Born in Preston, Lancashire, he grew up in that town and began a promising career as a journalist. He was also an excellent amateur pianist and when the New Victoria Cinema opened in 1928 with Leslie James as the solo organist he took lessons with him and quickly mastered the Wurlitzer organ installed there. Soon afterwards Reginald Foort appointed him as his assistant for the opening of the Regent, Bournemouth, and the New Victoria in London. Phil Park remained at the New Victoria when Foort left to take over from Quentin Maclean at the Regal, Marble Arch, and made two records on the large Compton organ before he, too, moved across to Marble Arch where he and Sidney Torch were employed as pianists and relief organists. In 1933 he was appointed solo organist at the Regal, West Norwood in South London, returning to Victoria again in 1935 to open the Wurlitzer at the Metropole Cinema. During this period he was developing a talent for lyric-writing - a skill which was to be fully exploited on joining Union Cinemas. He began by touring in the southern area, and then become resident at Kingston where he was put

Ritz Scunthorpe, showing the original console from the Super Gravesend. Photo: Tony Moss Collection.

Ritz Huddersfield, the first Union Wurlitzer, the only one with an illuminated seat. Photo: British Newspaper Library

Harold Ramsay broadcasting from the Union Kingston upon Thames.
Photo: Author's Collection.

Union Kingston upon Thames. Photo: Tony Moss Collection.

Ritz Oxford, pioneered the Union style of decor. Photo: Tony Moss Collection.

Regal Cowley, Oxford, the main foyer showing chandeliers and mirrors. Photo: Tony Moss Collection.

Union Cinemas Ritz Horsham.
Photo: Tony Moss Collection.

Ritz Woking, showing ornamental grille.
Photo: Tony Moss Collection.

Ritz Cleethorpes, with ornamental grille carried over ceiling.
Photo: Tony Moss Collection.

Ritz Belfast.
Photo: Tony Moss Collection.

Ritz Warrington.
Photo: John D. Sharp Collection.

Capitol Didsbury, Manchester.
Photo: Tony Moss Collection.

Barry Bretonner, Union Kingston.
Photo: Author's Collection.

Cecil Chadwick,
Ritz Barnsley,
Photo: Frank Hare
collection

Robinson Cleaver, Regal Bexley Heath.
Photo: John D. Sharp Collection.

Andreé Conti, Union Kingston.
Photo: Author's Collection.

in charge of the company's Music Department and also started to contribute a regular column in the house magazine.

For the week commencing 15 June, two more organists each made their first appearance. One of these was Andrée Conti at the Ritz, Tunbridge Wells, where she was billed as "The Famous Continental Star." Born on the French Riviera, she had pursued classical studies in Marseilles and later in Prague, later turning to music of a lighter kind and touring extensively in a number of European countries and broadcasting in some of them. At Union her presentation included piano, organ and xylophone - playing the latter instruments to her own (recorded) organ accompaniment when so desired. The second organist appeared at the Ritz, Huddersfield, and his name was Rudy Lewis. Another classical scholar, he had studied organ at the Royal College of Music and, like Allender Fryer, had taken lessons from Dr.G.D.Cunningham. Again, turning his attention to the lighter side, he became a pianist and accordionist with a tango band and then with other bands before specialising in the cinema organ.

All four of these organists quickly became important members of the Union team and in their different ways made a valuable contribution to the live entertainment presented by the company.

The month of June 1936 also saw the Head Office of the company settling in at new premises at 15 Regent Street in London's West End, to be known as "Union House." Originally, the headquarters had been located in Charing Cross Road, later moving to Wardour Street. As the company grew, additional premises were needed and eventually there were offices at 143, 167-69 and 197 Wardour Street, also Broadwick House in Broad Street and in Newman Street. Now, with the rapid expansion of the company, it was desirable that the various departments should be brought under one roof: they were listed as Film Booking, Variety Booking, Construction, Engineers, Catering, Estate, Accounts, Theatre Control, Publicity, Purchasing and what was described somewhat mysteriously as "Exploitation" - could that have been a catch-all term covering forward planning and future developments, for example the identification of sites for new cinemas and the negotiations pertaining thereto?

In mid-June it was announced that a new cinema would be built in Boston, Lincolnshire, to be a 1,646-seater with a 3-manual Compton organ. This was a project which did not materialise. A week later came confirmation that the Darlington scheme had been finally turned down.

The Macclesfield project, for a 1,457-seater with organ and large stage, was described as having been "deferred" - apparently because of objections from the local Highways Committee.

At Bognor Regis on the coast of West Sussex the company's plans for a 1,000-seater cinema were also turned down following objections from the local police on grounds of public safety arising, I believe, from concerns over the proposed location in relation to street traffic in the vicinity. It became fairly clear that this was one of the towns where Union were competing against Odeon Theatres and there was even a suggestion that Union sought to obtain an amalgamation with the Bognor Pier Company in an attempt to strengthen their bargaining position in the matter, but nothing came of it. The competition continued elsewhere - not least in Horsham where it gave rise to an extraordinary situation which I shall describe in the next chapter.

CHAPTER FOUR

COMPETITION & CONSOLIDATION

In the fullness of time it came to be recognised that the building of the Ritz, Horsham, was probably the most outstanding example of what could result from relentless competition with the Odeon chain. As we have seen, Union Cinemas had already acquired control of three cinemas in the town - the Capitol, Carfax and Winter Garden - none of which could realistically be described as modern. When it became known that Odeon, the arch-rivals, were planning to build a modern cinema in the town, the Directors resolved to build one as well and, moreover, to open it first. The result was, predictably, that once both the Ritz and the Odeon had been opened this relatively modest-sized town became greatly over-seated and Union were eventually obliged to close two of their other cinemas. The Ritz, incidentally, came under the ownership of the subsidiary company National Provincial Cinemas.

The Ritz was opened on Saturday 13 June 1936 by the Mayor and Mayoress in the company of a distinguished gathering of invited guests, including the actor Arthur Riscoe. The ceremony began with a fanfare by the Bach Trumpeters of the Royal Military School of Music. As on previous openings, Gaumont British cameramen were present to film the proceedings. A number of congratulatory messages were read out, including one from Jack Buchanan, star of "When Knights were Bold", the main feature film being presented. Harold Ramsay presided at the Compton organ and received a warm ovation.

The plans for the cinema were drawn up by L.H.Parsons FRIBA of the firm Goodman & Kay, with Verity & Beverley acting as consultants. Supervising the building and fitting out was J.H.Lundy, the Director of Theatre Construction. The plans had originally been laid before the local magistrates in December 1935 and were approved after certain modifications had been agreed. These included reducing the number of seats in the auditorium from 1,193 to 1,091. An organ had not been provided for, but one was nevertheless installed.

The exterior of the building was of local brick and stone and designed to harmonise with the surroundings, with the entrance doors surmounted by recessed windows, the treatment of the facade giving what was described as "an adaptation of Georgian design to modern practice." The spacious entrance hall was decorated in mahogany and gold, whilst reds, browns and gold were strongly featured in the auditorium, with concealed lighting in the ceiling. The projection room equipment included Kalee projectors and Western Electric sound apparatus.

The organ was the first of a new type to be developed by Compton, intended for use in smaller cinemas with seating for around 1,000 patrons. It was of 2 manuals and 4 pipe units only (The usual Tibia and Flute, together with string tone supplied by a Gamba and reed tone in the form of a versatile Tromba instead of the more customary Tuba) supplemented by the patent Melotone electronic unit, installed in a single chamber under the stage. The swell shutters were vertical and fitted with individual shutter motors instead of the standard Compton whiffletree system by which the shutters were actuated by a single large motor. The console was as usual mounted on a lift and fitted with a "Rainbow" illuminated surround, so that all the standard aids to presentation were present. It is interesting to note that Harold Ramsay had been appearing at the Ritz, Huddersfield, during the week but travelled down specially for the Horsham opening on the Saturday: evidently he attached considerable importance to the launch of this new model. It is not altogether clear whether he was involved as a design consultant, as he had only joined Union Cinemas the previous month. It is certainly possible that he was involved, of course, just as he had been in respect of the Wurlitzer organ for the Ritz, Huddersfield, some considerable time before joining the company and the organ did possess features which suggested Ramsay's influence. Another interesting possibility, suggested to me in recent days by former Union organist Arthur Lord, is that J.I. Taylor, Technical Director of the John Compton Organ Co., may have felt that the standard 3-manual 6-unit model in regular production could be improved upon, offering better value for money, by working with a smaller specification but with superior pipework and voicing. At Horsham, Ramsay made just the one appearance on the Saturday evening. Pierson Webber was the featured organist for the next two weeks, Harold Ramsay himself appearing at the Ritz, Oxford, for the first week and at the Luxor, Eastbourne for the second.

Later, when the opening of the Odeon, Horsham, was announced to take place on 7 October, the advertisement in the local press occupied a modest 6 inches across two columns; on the same page, the Ritz block occupied no less than 15 inches across four columns! This carried the headline "Horsham Goes Crazy" and announced the personal appearance of Harold Ramsay at the organ, a stage show featuring Archie and his Famous Juvenile Band, and Charlie Chaplin in "Modern Times" on the screen. In addition, at the Winter Gardens and Carfax cinemas the admission to matinée performances (except Saturdays) would be reduced to tuppence and threepence and to threepence, sixpence and ninepence in the evenings! Competitiveness indeed!

The next new cinema to be opened was the Ritz, Penzance, the ceremony being performed by the Mayor and Mayoress on 27 July, with Harold Ramsay at the organ. The local press, reporting the event, said "One attraction the Ritz alone possesses among cinemas in Cornwall is what is known as the Mighty Organ. The services of Mr Harold Ramsay, famous for his organ broadcasts, were secured for the opening of this wonderful instrument, and the audience were so charmed by his renditions that his selections had to be prolonged." Not all local newspaper reporters wrote like that in those days, but a fair number did!

The new cinema was located in Queen Street and was designed by A.H.Jones FRIBA. The entrance was situated to the right of the main frontage, with the cream and green canopy extending along the full length. The doors were in black with red fillets. The name "Ritz" was carried on a vertical fin projecting from the face of the building and fitted with neon lighting. The decoration of the entrance hall and auditorium was carried out in a range of reds speckled over in metallic gold. Lighting was provided by three attractive units on either side of the auditorium, together with two concealed lighting troughs in the ceiling The proscenium surround was of fibrous plaster, with the top section incorporating a grille opening for the organ to speak through from its chamber located above the stage. The 1,000 seats in the auditorium were in salmon pink. The projection room was equipped, as usual, with Kalee projectors and Western Electric sound system.

The organ was the second of the new Compton models to be built with 2 manuals and 4 pipe units plus the Melotone unit and "Rainbow" illuminated surround for the lift-mounted console. The specification was virtually identical to that of the Horsham instrument, but with the organ chamber this time located above the stage rather than below it. Harold Ramsay stayed for the whole of the first week, after which a pattern of residencies lasting four or five weeks emerged, presumably because of the distance visiting organists had to travel to appear there. Neville Meale undertook the first of these, but told me recently that as Penzance was regarded as a holiday resort it became Union policy to change the film programme twice weekly to encourage return visits to the cinema, this in turn involving organists in having to prepare two different slide shows each week! However, Alex Taylor was featured for one week only commencing 7 September and he was followed for one week by Pearce Bowden FRCO, a Professor at Trinity College, London, who had been specially engaged in July to tour the circuit with a presentation of classical music intended to demonstrate the versatility of the cinema organ. After that, the next short-term residency fell to Jack Dowle.

It was during Harold Ramsay's visit to Penzance that he first met Dudley Savage, at that time a 16-year-old who had just won First Prize in an open competition for organ-playing. He was greatly impressed by the young man's ability and saw the possibility of touring him as "The Cornish Wonder Boy Organist." After a period of coaching, Dudley was launched on his new career in January 1937, initially at Penzance and then at Kingston before setting out on a major tour of the circuit. Quite often he was accompanied by one or more vocalists, usually as youthful as himself. Some time later, after Associated British Cinemas had acquired control of Union Cinemas, Dudley Savage was posted to the Royal, Plymouth, the fine Compton organ of which had been opened by Wilfred Southworth on 15 July 1938, and was to remain resident there for many years. It was during this period that he devised what was to become one of the longest-running series of broadcast request programmes, "As Prescribed" - intended mainly for the benefit of hospital patients and with the dedications introduced by himself. Happily, at the time of writing, Dudley Savage is still with us and entertaining the various cinema organ clubs and societies throughout the country.

During this period a number of announcements were made in the trade press regarding the construction of new cinemas and the acquisition of new sites and these included the following:

Plans for the building of a new Ritz at the junction of Ellis Street and Lord Street in Keighley were approved by the Keighley Urban District

Council. The architects appointed were Verity & Beverley. In the event, this cinema was not opened until after Associated British Cinemas had taken over control of Union Cinemas.

Another new cinema was planned to be built on the site of the covered market at Urmston, Manchester, Verity & Beverley again being appointed as architects. Further north, at Rawtenstall, another scheme was adjourned by local magistrates sine die.

In Swansea a site in Singleton Street was to be cleared by the firm of Bennett (Bros.) Contractors Ltd., but evidently a lengthy delay ensued thereafter. It would appear that considerable difficulty was encountered in awarding a building contract in this instance.

At Bedminster, Bristol, a 1,792-seater cinema was planned to be erected in North Street, but here also there was a considerable delay and ultimately the opening did not take place until December 1940, long after the demise of Union Cinemas.

An application to build at Aberdare was refused pending agreement over sites, plans, etc.

An extraordinary event occurred in August when William Southan Morris, General Manager of the Company, returned from holiday in America and was immediately called in to a meeting of directors and summarily dismissed from his post. Obviously this came to him as a great shock, as before his departure on holiday his relationship with the directors had been most cordial and they had indeed wished him "bon voyage." Now he was accused of a whole catalogue of failings in the execution of his managerial duties. In the circumstances, it was hardly surprising that he decided to sue the Company for wrongful dismissal: the case did not come to court until November 1937, when it was heard by no less than the Lord Chief Justice himself, with Mr Morris represented by the great Sir Patrick Hastings. The case was won and substantial damages were awarded. I will refer to the case again in more detail in a later chapter.

Today one can only speculate as to what really went on behind the scenes, but it could be that there was a general redistribution of functions including the abolition of the post of General Manager.

Part and parcel of the changes certainly included the promotion of Harold Ramsay to the newly-created post of Controller of

Entertainment, putting him in overall charge of the whole of the live entertainment offered by the Company. In addition to responsibility for the musical direction involving the organs and organists which he already held, he now took on board the stage presentations generally - leading in due course to variety broadcasts by top-class artistes and a host of other promotions. As an organist himself, Harold Ramsay recommenced broadcasting on 21 August, from the Regal, Kingston, thereafter going on the air every 7-10 days. As already mentioned, he also continued his recording contract on the Parlophone label, the first of his several recordings on the Kingston organ being issued during the same month.

Towards the end of the month the appointment was announced of V. Hayes-Jones as Assistant to Harold Ramsay. He had worked with the organ-builders Hill, Norman & Beard and had been involved in the introduction of the Christie Unit Organ in the 1920s, moving to the Wurlitzer organisation in November 1935. He was also a Director of the Wardour Musical and Variety Agency.

A presentation which was conceived about this time was "Great Moments from the Opera" in which well-known operatic stars would be featured in scenes from some of the best-known operas, accompanied by a small orchestra backed by the organ and with suitable stage settings and lighting. A start was made, but it did not appear to be very successful and was quickly dropped.

In September it was announced that a link-up with the Paramount group of cinemas was to be made, whereby Paramount Theatres would take control of the day-to-day management of both organisations. Leslie Holderness as Theatre Controller would head the team of Paramount executives working at Union House, thereby taking pressure off the Union Management who were by now heavily preoccupied with the expansion programme. They would deal with all operations except film bookings, with special emphasis on the variety acts presented on stage - these would in future be joint bookings for both circuits, the agency involved being Montague Lyon Ltd., of which Frederick Bernhard was Managing Director.

In addition to the six cinemas already controlled by Union Cinemas in Barrow-in-Furness (The Regal, Coliseum, Pavilion, Gaiety, Palace and Walney) the Company decided to acquire another! This cinema had been newly-built as an entirely local enterprise by one Mr Brennan, to plans drawn up by architects Drury & Gomersall, and was to have been called the Roxy. However, it was sold to Union Cinemas only a few weeks before the Opening, thus completing their monopoly in the town.

The Ritz was opened by the Mayor on 14 September in the presence of the Mayoress, David Bernhard, Frederick Bernhard, Leslie Holderness and other officials of the Company, together with James Brennan, the architect Joseph Gomersall and others connected with the original project. The proceedings began with a fanfare provided by trumpeters of the King's Own Royal Regiment and the Barrow Shipyard Band, ranged on either side of the stage. Guests were then introduced and welcomed by Mr Kirkby who was General Manager of the Company's cinemas in the town, after which a series of light-hearted speeches were made. Much was made of the fact that the site of the new cinema, though in a prominent position, had previously been waste ground covered in litter and refuse and generally considered a local eyesore. Mr Brennan had done the town a great service by clearing it and erecting a fine modern 1,735-seater cinema in its place.

Alex Taylor was the organist chosen to perform for the opening cere-mony and he remained at Barrow for the first three weeks. In due course he was followed by Neville Meale who at the time appeared to be next in the pecking order after Taylor. After him came Joseph Seal, resident at the Lonsdale, Carlisle, and broadcasting regularly from that cinema, though he had already made occasional appearances else-where - in particular at the Ritz, Huddersfield. In due course Harold Ramsay was to appear at Barrow for the week commencing 23 November, direct from the highly successful broadcast opening of the Ritz, Belfast, and the two-week run which followed it, including another broadcast. However, we are running ahead - details of all this will be given in the next chapter!

The Barrow organ itself was a Compton standard model of 3 manuals and 6 pipe units with Melotone, of which many examples were built, with minor variations, from 1935 onwards. The "Rainbow" style of illu-minated surround was fitted to the console.

Organists newly appointed during this period included the following:

Edward Farley, who started at the Majestic, Gravesend, on 31 August. A native of Kent, he had studied organ at Canterbury Cathedral and at the Conservatoire Nationale in Paris before turning to cinema work in 1921. He brought a wealth of experience to Union Cinemas.

Another important arrival on 31 August was Arthur Manning, apparently "doubling" the Ritz, Huddersfield, and the Regal, Dewsbury during that week. Subsequently, he toured the circuit extensively.

Cecil Chadwick, a Lancastrian whose career began in the days of silent films and included appointments at the Trocadero, Southport, the Plaza, Stockport, and the Classic, Belfast, was appointed to the Capitol, Didsbury, commencing 21 September. As he had been broadcasting regularly from Belfast, with more than two hundred transmissions to his credit, the plan was to cash in on his popularity by appointing him to the Ritz, Belfast, by now fast approaching completion. In the event, this did not happen - though he did appear there - but he became the Company's chief organist in the North, touring the cinemas in the region and continuing regular broadcasts from Didsbury.

In a press release published on 20 August 1936 David Bernhard, Chairman, announced that major changes in the financial arrangements of the three Companies would be proposed in the near future. In due course, the restructuring programme was made known: the Union Cinema Co. Ltd., Oxford & Berkshire Cinemas Ltd. and National Provincial Cinemas Ltd. would be wound up and replaced by a single company to be known as Union Cinemas Ltd. The extraordinary general meetings required for this purpose would take place on 27 November.

CHAPTER FIVE

A NEW COMPANY "IN TOWN TONIGHT"

In the early days of its expansion programme, as we have seen, the Union Cinema Co. often became involved in new cinema projects initiated by others. In due course this was to apply to what would be opened as the Ritz, Belfast. It had originally been planned by another important figure in the world of cinema-building, Lou Morris, but was taken over by Union at an early stage of construction; it was to become one of the key cinemas on the circuit. The Ritz was officially opened on 9 November by the Lord Mayor of Belfast, Sir Crawford McCullagh, before a distinguished gathering which included the High Sheriff and almost the entire City Council. David Bernhard, Chairman, and Frederick Bernhard, Managing Director, together with other directors and officials of the Union Cinema Company were present on stage. It certainly was one of the most important achievements of the Company to date. A pleasing touch was the presentation of a gold key to the Lord Mayor by Leslie Kemp, the architect. The celebrities invited to attend and take part in the stage show included Gracie Fields and Jack Hylton and his Band, with Jack Hylton acting as compere.

The importance of the occasion was underlined by the fact that the stage show presented at the Opening (and retained for the first two weeks) was broadcast by the BBC on the Northern Ireland wavelength. The show included Sony Farrar and his Band, the comedians Bennett and McNaughton, the Gordon Ray Girls (from Radiolympia) and Harold Ramsay at the organ.

The Ritz was designed by three men working in close collaboration: Leslie H. Kemp ARIBA, E. F. Tulley LRIBA (The Company's staff

Architect) and J. H. Lundy (Director of Theatre Construction). The building was located on the corner of College Square East and Grosvenor Road, with faience-covered facades and full-length canopies in both directions. On the corner itself was a tower bearing a vertical name sign. Marble steps led up from street level to the swing doors leading into the draught lobby and thence into the main foyer, a dramatic feature of which was the grand staircase leading to the balcony and café. The café, measuring 80 feet by 30 feet, included a maple floor laid down for dancing. the auditorium had seating for 2,500 patrons. The well-equipped stage was 76 feet wide overall and 28 feet deep and was served by a scenery dock and property, dressing and rehearsal rooms.

Another important feature was the Compton organ, the only 4-manual organ to be installed new by the Company. It was one of a number of models of this type built by Compton from 1934 onwards having 10 pipe units, the fourth manual being a coupler manual. Some of the early examples also had the "Solo Cello" attachment, in which the string was "bowed" and the fingering was achieved by mechanical means, the result being amplified through a loudspeaker. As noted earlier, one of these devices was fitted to the Compton 3-manual organ installed at the Ritz, Tunbridge Wells in 1934 another was to be found at the Regal, Bexley Heath. However, production of the "Solo Cello" was discontinued in 1935 in favour of the Melotone electronic unit, the Belfast organ being one of those so equipped. In addition, a "phantom" grand piano attachment was placed on the right hand side of the stage. Another interesting feature of this organ was the new type of illuminated surround for the console, manufactured by R. R. Beard Ltd. a firm of illumination engineers located just off the Old Kent Road in south-east London. Sometimes referred to as the "Pillar and Vase" style of surround, this eventually became standard for all the Company's new organs - Compton and Wurlitzer alike - and an improved version was introduced later on. Thus, another new feature was added to those already existing to distinguish the Union circuit from others. The organ chambers were situated under the stage.

This particular organ was certainly one of the finest cinema instruments to be built by Compton and continued to be broadcast for many years to come. With the take-over of the Ritz project by Union Cinemas one may wonder if the organ was outstanding because of pressure on the builders from Harold Ramsay or because Comptons were aware of the company's increasing interest in placing orders for Wurlitzers and were therefore keen to do a really good job in the expectation of securing more orders for themselves. There was also the likelihood that it would be used regularly for broadcasts on the Northern Ireland Regional wavelength and possibly on the National Programme as well - as indeed proved to be the case.

Mention may be made of another feature of the opening programme: "In Town Tonight", based on the BBC Saturday evening broadcasts of that name. The idea was to present brief interviews with interesting local personalities and in Belfast these included one Jim Salmon, said to be the oldest riveter in the town, Jenny King, a well-known flower seller, and John Geddes, the oldest jaunting-car driver (whatever that is!), among others. The "In Town Tonight" feature was adopted for several other openings in succeeding months.

In mid-October the trade press announced what was undoubtedly one of the most significant appointments to date: that of Sidney Torch, who made his first appearance for the Company week commencing 16 November at the Regal, Kingston. He had built up a huge following as organist at the Regal, Marble Arch, in 1932-34 and at the Regal, Edmonton, from 1934 onwards. His style of playing, particularly of "hot" numbers, was unlike anything that had been attempted previously on the cinema organ and had attracted the attention of the record companies. He made a large number of records for the Columbia label at both cinemas and the "hotter" the performances the better they sold. In addition, he had broadcast regularly from Edmonton and had established a reputation as one of the best-known cinema organists of the period. As well as his broadcasts for the BBC he had a regular weekly programme with a guest artiste (a singer or instrumentalist) for commercial radio on Radio Luxembourg, repeated a few days later on Radio Normandy; the sponsors were the makers of Robinson's Lemon Barley Water. There can be little doubt that Union Cinemas offered him a substantial increase in salary to tempt him to join the Company. After one week at Kingston, he set out on tour starting with three weeks at the Ritz, Belfast, from where he recommenced his broadcasting for the BBC.

Also on 16 November the Yorkshire-born organist Douglas Walker appeared for the first time at the Regal, St. Leonards. After early academic training leading to LRAM and ARCM diplomas and experience as a church organist, he turned to the cinema to accompany silent films and later studied the cinema organ with Harry Davidson. He was thus very well qualified to join the Union circuit and was particularly useful in the accompaniment of stage shows.

Another important addition to the team was James Bell ARCM, making his first appearance at the Ritz, Horsham, for the two weeks commencing 30 November; this was followed by a week at the Regal, Kingston, before proceeding to the Northern area where his tour included a three-week stint at the Ritz, Huddersfield. James Bell was yet another organist with a formal classical training who had taken up cinema work. He was already widely known through regular broadcasts from the Carlton, Tuebrook, Liverpool. Later, after leaving Union, he was to open the magnificent 5-manual Compton organ at the Odeon, Leicester Square, and become the first resident organist at that important West End cinema.

The broadcast of the stage show at the opening of the Ritz, Belfast, may have been a "trial run" for more broadcasts of this kind. At any rate, there was a more ambitious variety show at the Regal, Kingston, described in the local press advertisement as a "World Broadcast" on 15 December. The bill included Clapham and Dwyer, Norman Long, Stanley Holloway, Gypsy Nina and Harold Ramsay at the organ. However, in the Radio Times the well-known impressionist Florence Desmond was billed instead of Stanley Holloway. This broadcast from Kingston was to be the first of several which were to follow in 1937.

On 27 November extraordinary general meetings were held in connection with the financial reorganisation first announced by David Bernhard in August, whereby the existing companies were to be wound up and a new consolidated company launched. The meetings involved the Union Cinema Co. Ltd. (the £350,000 parent company), National Provincial Cinemas Ltd. (a £750,000 associate) and Oxford & Berkshire Cinemas Ltd. (a £350,000 associate). The assets of these companies upon winding up were to be sold in consideration for shares in the new company, to be known as Union Cinemas Ltd. Preference shareholders in the old companies would receive allocations of shares in the new company carrying the right to fixed preferential dividends equivalent to the maximum income to which they were currently entitled. Holders of ordinary shares in the old companies would receive allocations of shares in the new company, having regard to the current and anticipated earnings of each of the old companies as reviewed by the directors.

The authorised capital of Union Cinemas Ltd. was to be £6,500,000 (compared to the old combined total of £1,450,000). This would be made up of £2,000,000 in Redeemable 6 per cent Cumulative First Preference shares of £1 each, £1,500,000 in Redeemable 6 per cent

Second Preference shares of £1 each, £2,500,000 in 10,000,000 "A" Ordinary shares of 5s.0d. each, and £500,000 in 2,000,000 Ordinary shares of 5s.0d. each

The First and Second Preference shares were to be redeemable in 1940 at 22s.0d. or at the Company's options at 23s.0d. any time after 31 December 1938.

I believe it is important that I should set out the new arrangements in clear detail as they were relevant to the subsequent fortunes of the new company, as will become clear later. The allocation of new shares in exchange for holdings in the old companies was as follows:

Union Cinema Co. Ltd:
For every six 7 per cent Cumulative Participating Preference shares of £1: five 6 per cent Cumulative First Preference shares of £1 each and five 6 per cent Cumulative Second Preference shares of £1 each.

For every Ordinary share of £1: thirty-seven "A" Ordinary shares of 5s.0d. each and twelve Ordinary shares of 5s.0d. each.

National Provincial Cinemas Ltd:
For every twenty-four 6 per cent Cumulative Participating Preference shares of 5s.0d.: seventeen 6 per cent Cumulative Participating First Preference shares of £1 each and seventeen 6 per cent Cumulative Participating Second Preference shares of £1 each.

For each Ordinary share of 5s.0d.: three "A" Ordinary shares of 5s.0d. each and one Ordinary share of 5s.0d.

Oxford & Berkshire Cinemas Ltd:
For each 7 per cent Cumulative Participating Preference share of £1: one 6 per cent Cumulative First Preference share of £1 and one 6 per cent Second Preference share of £1.

For each Ordinary share of 5s.0d.: two "A" Ordinary shares of 5s.0d. each and one Ordinary share of 5s.0d.

When these proposed arrangements were approved, the issued capital of the new company would amount to £3,169,237 compared with the issued capital of the three old companies of £1,414,891. This would leave approximately £3,330,000 available for further extensions as desired.

The Directors of the new company were to be David Bernhard (Chairman), Frederick Bernhard (Managing Director) and Lawrence Clements.

It was pointed out that the consolidation would produce several advantages, including improved opportunities for profitable expansion, achievement of working economies and access to a wider market on the Stock Exchange than had been possible under the old regime.

At the Annual General Meeting held on 23 November David Bernhard told shareholders that the estimated profits of the consolidated company for the full year would be approximately £240,000 - sufficient to cover the dividend on the new First Preference shares more than six times over and then leaving enough to cover the Second Preference shares more than five times; the balance still remaining would be equivalent to more than 8 per cent on the new A" Ordinary and Ordinary shares. It was reported that the shareholders present appeared to be well satisfied with this information and with the arrangements proposed for setting up the new company. Apparently no questions were asked and the Chairman's report was accepted unanimously - which in retrospect might seem a little surprising. In due course the manner of the capital reconstruction would come to be described as involving "share inflation" but there was as yet no recognition of this. So the new company, Union Cinemas Ltd., was registered on 16 December 1936.

It would appear that the former associate companies continued to operate as subsidiaries alongside the others, as responsibility for several of the cinemas was shifted from one to another. For example, the Regal, Bexley Heath, the Lonsdale, Carlisle and the Rivoli, Southend, were placed with National Provincial Cinemas. Again, a number of cinemas were transferred to another subsidiary company, Alliance Cinemas Limited, including the following:

Regal, Altrincham	Capitol, Didsbury
Regal Beckenham	Broadway, Eccles
Regal Yarmouth	Kingsway, Levenshulme
Union, Kingston	Alma, Luton

Interestingly, the Kingston cinema was listed as the "Union" - so evidently the decision to rename this flagship cinema had already been taken. However, the actual change of name did not take place until the first weekend in March 1937, suggesting that it took time to obtain the new lettering and lighting for the exterior signs and so forth.

As previously indicated, in several cases where existing cinemas had been acquired, works were put in hand to refurbish them, including to a greater or lesser extent modifications to the building, redecoration of the interior and other desirable changes to improve them and bring them up to a higher standard. One such cinema was the Rivoli at Southend, where it was considered desirable to modernise the property, bearing in mind the town's importance as a popular seaside resort. The building itself dated from 1896 and was reconstructed as a cinema to the plans of George Coles in 1920, known at different times as the Alexander and the Empire.

Work at Southend apparently proceeded day and night in order to meet the deadline for the reopening of the cinema on 28 December. In addition to the complete redecoration of the interior, the original Christie Unit Organ of 2 manuals and 8 pipe units installed in 1928 was rebuilt and enlarged to 3 manuals and 10 units by the Wurlitzer Company who also supplied a wooden console surround bearing a strong resemblance to the house style adopted by the Granada circuit!

The advertisement in the local press announcing the reopening was headed "The Dawn of a New Era in Cinema Entertainment" and carried the footnote "You dare not miss this outstanding event in the annals of Southend's Entertainment!" This rather extravagant type of publicity was becoming increasingly common practice. Apart from the two feature films, the programme included Harold Ramsay at the organ and a stage show which included Stanelli, described as "the famous BBC Stag Party Comedian." Among other talents, Stanelli used to perform on what he called his "Hornchestra" - a tuned set of thirty or so old-fashioned motor horns on which popular tunes could be played in a somewhat grotesque manner. Also in the bill was Van Dock, the comedy cartoonist who was a Royal Command performer and had appeared in London and at the Folies Bergère in Paris. Two other speciality acts completed the programme and thus did the new-look Rivoli get off to a good start. In the ensuing weeks Robinson Cleaver, Sidney Torch and Alex Taylor followed Harold Ramsay at the organ.

At the end of December plans were announced for a new Ritz to be built at Blackburn at a cost of £70,000 and an artist's impression of the proposed building was published in the trade press. However, Union Cinemas apparently did not proceed with this project and later a company called Northern Theatres Co. Ltd. were reported to be inviting tenders for it.

Very important to the entertainment business was the holiday town of Blackpool and a huge development was announced by the Company: this was to comprise a 4,000-seat cinema with café, ballroom and underground car park, located at the junction of Adelaide Street and Leopold Grove and planned by Drury & Gomersall. Again, this also came to nothing. A 1,000-seater for Ripon, employing the same architects, was also planned, and further references were made by the Company to its intention to erect a large cinema in Swansea. A site for a cinema in Bishop Auckland was also said to have been acquired and, a little earlier, plans were mentioned for a cinema in Kirkgate Market in Bradford, to be drawn up by Verity & Beverley and built by A.Segal. This may have been listed in the building programme announced at the beginning of the year, but again no further information was forthcoming.

It will be seen that Union Cinemas certainly had exceedingly ambitious plans at this time, but that by no means all of them actually came to fruition.

After the broadcast of the stage show at the Opening Night of the Ritz, Belfast, on 9 November, other broadcasts by visiting organists followed in quick succession. To the end of the year, these were as follows:

Date	Time	Organist	Wavelength
19.11.36	8.45	Harold Ramsay	Northern Ireland
3.12.36	7.30	Sidney Torch	Northern Ireland
10.12.36	6.40	Sidney Torch	Northern Ireland
24.12.36	7.30	Alex Taylor	Northern Ireland
26.12.36	11.0	Alex Taylor	National
31.12.36	9.00	Alex Taylor	Northern Ireland

Broadcasts of this frequency were to continue into the New Year.

CHAPTER SIX

"RADIO RODEO" ROPES IN THE AUDIENCES

1937 started well with the Opening on 4 January of the Ritz, Ipswich, the ceremony being performed as usual by the town's Mayor. Leslie Holderness, the company's Theatre Controller, welcomed the Mayor and Mayoress and made a short speech outlining Union Cinemas' policy of building modern cinemas in towns such as Ipswich and thereby contributing significantly to the entertainment amenities on offer locally. Also present on the stage were E.R.Adams and his wife and other Company officials. Special guests for the occasion were the film star Anna Neagle and her husband, the producer Herbert Wilcox, but unfortunately they were delayed and did not arrive until about 9.30.pm. However, a large crowd awaited them outside and with powerful lighting their arrival was filmed for showing at the cinema in due course.

Following the actual opening ceremony came the "In Town Tonight" feature, introduced by Harold Ramsay. First to appear were some of the men who had taken part in the building of the Ritz; they were followed by Mr O'Brien, Manager of the Ipswich Town Football Club. Then came Herbert Wilcox who introduced Anna Neagle. Finally, the cinema's uniformed staff marched onto the stage, together with a band of girl pipers who - perhaps rather curiously - played "Auld Lang Syne" - the audience standing and joining hands as they sang.

Harold Ramsay's organ interlude took the form of a musical biography of his life as an organist, but starting with his early years in Norwich. The lavish stage show featured the well-known comedians Clapham and Dwyer, Macari and his Dutch Accordion Serenaders, Van Dock the cartoonist and the Eight Step Sisters. Later, a reception was held for the principal guests.

The cinema was located in the Buttermarket on the site of the old "Waggon and Horses" inn adjoining the Ancient House, formerly the departure point for the coach to London, and special care was taken by the architect and builders to protect this valuable old building as the work proceeded. The architect was Robert Cromie, assisted by E.F Tulley the Company's staff architect, the whole venture being supervised by J.H.Lundy the Director of Theatre Construction. Because of the narrowness of the Buttermarket, the actual building line was set back so that the pavement outside could also be set back to provide a lay-by for cars dropping off or picking up patrons. In addition, there was no canopy over the entrance, the doors themselves being inset. The exterior of the building was faced with dull red bricks and stone to achieve an agreeable harmony with its surroundings.

The interior of the Ritz was decorated discreetly, the treatment of the spacious entrance hall, café-restaurant (featuring a spectacular crystal chandelier) and 1,689-seat auditorium creating an atmosphere of richness and warmth, with soft, concealed lighting adding to the feeling of quiet luxury. The well-equipped stage provided all the facilities required for the presentation of live entertainment in line with the Company's established policy of Cine-Variety.

The organ was the second Wurlitzer to be purchased new by the Company and the first since Harold Ramsay's appointment. Its specification to a large extent resembled that of the Ritz, Huddersfield, but with three changes in the list of pipe units employed (The keen Viole d'Orchestre and Celeste being replaced by the broader-toned Gamba and Celeste and the Vox Humana being replaced by a Saxophone unit) together with the useful addition of a general crescendo pedal. There was of course the all-important "phantom" grand piano on the stage. The illuminated surround for the console was of the "Rainbow" type rather than the new "Pillar and Vase" model first seen at the Ritz, Belfast. After the opening week, Robinson Cleaver appeared for the next two weeks and was followed by Andrée Conti, Sidney Torch and Alex Taylor, all for one week each. Thereafter, several other organists appeared, but Harold Ramsay himself did not return to Ipswich during the remaining period of the Company's existence.

On 18 January another new cinema was opened: the Ritz at Bexhill. This was a 1,142-seater designed by Verity & Beverley to typical Union standards. Unfortunately, its location in Buckhurst Road was not ideal, being some distance from the town centre, although its sky sign was visible from Devonshire Road, the main shopping thoroughfare. There was also considerable competition from three other cinemas in the town. The Ritz was not equipped with an organ; had there been one of, say the Compton 2-manual 4-unit models as introduced at Horsham, this might have proved an attractive addition to the cinema's drawing power. The Company could almost be said to have been in competition with itself by reason of its existing cinemas at nearby Eastbourne and St. Leonards.

The Compton 2-manual 4-unit model might have been an appropriate choice for the 1,000-seater cinema planned to be built at Retford and announced in the trade press in February. However, this proved to be one of those Union schemes which came to nothing.

An important opening did take place on 27 February at Scunthorpe, when the town's Member of Parliament officiated. The celebrity guest was Ann Penn and Alex Taylor presided at the organ. Located in the Doncaster Road, the Ritz was designed by Robert Cromie assisted by Staff Architect E.F.Tulley working to the requirements of Director of Theatre Construction J.H.Lundy.

The building was faced with red bricks and stone dressings and an unusual feature was an ornamental pylon standing well forward from the main facade and bearing the neon-lit name "RITZ". The decorative scheme in the vestibule created an atmosphere of warmth and luxury, enhanced by mirrors and brilliant lighting. The feeling of luxury was carried forward into the auditorium where warm tones of dull rose pink and pastel shades were relieved by old gold. Being in the 1,000-seater class, all the seating was on one level with no balcony. The seats themselves were upholstered in a soft salmon-coloured velvet. Concealed lighting was used to illuminate the auditorium. For a relatively small cinema, the stage was quite large and well equipped and accommodation was provided for dressing rooms and scenery storage. "Simplex" projection and the B.T.H. sound system were adopted, the latter featuring "extended frequency range" for the best possible sound reproduction.

The organ installed at Scunthorpe was in fact the Compton 3-manual 5-unit instrument originally at the Super, Gravesend, but removed after the Company acquired the Majestic in that town and began to feature the larger Compton in that cinema. Thus it had the early "Cascade" type of illuminated console surround, complete with bench, with which it had been fitted at Gravesend. Alex Taylor remained for the first three weeks, being followed by Pierson Webber, Andrée Conti and Joseph Seal, all of whom had three-week stints. Harold Cryer arrived week commencing 5 July to become the first resident organist at Scunthorpe. Prior to that he had spent seven weeks at the Ritz, Barrow, and he returned there for a further four weeks from 13 September. From time to time other guest organists appeared at Scunthorpe, including Sidney Torch, Neville Meale and Gordon Banner.

At the beginning of March the Ritz, Newtownards, Co. Down, was opened by Miss E.M.Montgomery, member of the local Board of Guardians and Rural District Council. This cinema was a complete reconstruction of the old Picture Palace and was designed by R.Sharpe Hill of Belfast, under the direction of J.H.Lundy. The exterior was finished in cream-coloured faience on a black base, with a "Snowcrete" finish above. The vestibule was laid with terrazzo in a novel design and the auditorium had seating for 713 patrons. The entire projection department was equipped by Gaumont-British Equipment Ltd. and included the British Acoustic Sound System.

The climax of the period under review occurred on 22 March with the simultaneous opening of two new major cinemas: the Ritz, Chatham, and the Ritz, Barnsley. By means of a direct telephone link and the loudspeaker system, the actor Jack Buchanan could be heard by the audiences in both cinemas. The Daily Mirror of that day carried a Union Cinemas advertisement publicising the event.

The Opening Ceremony at the Ritz, Chatham, was performed by the Mayor of Chatham, accompanied by the Mayoress. Also present were the Mayor and Mayoress of neighbouring Gillingham and the star celebrity Jack Buchanan, together with directors of Union Cinemas and other distinguished guests. On stage were the Trumpeters and Drummers of the Royal Marines Band and the Dagenham Girl Pipers. Billy Cotton and his Band provided the stage show. Harold Ramsay was at the organ and in addition to his own presentation he introduced the popular "In Town Tonight", by now an established feature of the major Openings.

The new cinema was situated in the High Street and was designed by Robert Cromie in conjunction with E.F.Tulley. To improve the access for patrons, the frontage was set back 8 ft. from the building line.

Because of this, it was felt that the architectural possibilities of the facade were somewhat limited, but a pleasing effect was achieved using white stone, a symmetrical window design, illuminated canopy and walnut entrance doors. A large café-restaurant was built over the main vestibule. The auditorium, stated to be the largest in Kent with 2,322 seats, was decorated in peach speckled with gold and details were picked out in crimson and metal effects. Drapes were used on either side of the main grilles, the organ chambers being located behind the one on the left hand side facing the stage, while the proscenium arch itself was of simple design. An interesting feature of the auditorium was the set of eight inverted light fittings, four to each side. A full working stage was provided, together with a suite of dressing rooms and a scenery dock. The projection equipment included two Simplex projectors and Western Electric sound system with non-synchronous attachment, together with Bi-unial slide lantern and two spotlights.

The Wurlitzer organ was of particular interest, being an improved version of the one supplied for the Ritz, Ipswich: instead of the third manual being of the coupler type with its somewhat limited scope, in this case the layout was fully unified over all three manuals and there were additional controls available to the organist, including general pistons affecting the stops to be drawn on all manuals and pedal board. Another unique feature was the grand piano attachment mounted on its own lift alongside the console lift in the orchestra pit, rather than being placed on the stage; an architect's drawing still in existence seems to indicate that this innovation was something of an afterthought. The organ chambers were situated one above the other on the left hand side of the auditorium. The illuminated surround for the console was of the new "Pillar and Vase" type which had been introduced at Belfast.

Again, the Opening Ceremony at the Ritz, Barnsley, was performed by the Mayor, accompanied by the Mayoress, together with Mr. and Mrs. Beverley (representing the firm of Verity & Beverley, the architects) and Leslie Holderness, the Theatre Controller. As mentioned above, there was a direct telephone link with Chatham, so that the audiences in both cinemas could hear the proceedings through the loudspeaker systems; in particular, the Barnsley audience could hear Jack Buchanan addressing them from the stage at Chatham.

The Ritz was situated in Peel Street, with easy access from the main thoroughfares. Designed by Verity & Beverley in conjunction with E.F.Tulley and to the requirements specified by J.H.Lundy, the frontage was of stone. Entry was by a double line of glass doors, thus providing an effective draught lobby, and a feature of the spacious vestibule was a palatial two-way staircase leading to the balcony. The large auditorium, with seating for 2,007 patrons, was decorated in shades of terra-cotta, peach and gold. The stage was large and well-equipped, with ample dressing room accommodation. The projection room was up to the usual high standard of equipment and the cinema had the distinction of being the 2,000th to be fitted with Western Electric sound apparatus, this fact being commemorated by the unveiling of a special plaque in the vestibule.

Unfortunately, the Wurlitzer organ was not ready in time for the Opening and was the subject of a separate ceremony on 26 April ("The Show all Barnsley has been waiting for!" ran the advertisement in the local paper) when the Deputy-Mayor officiated and Robinson Cleaver was the featured organist. A stage show was also presented. The organ itself was similar to the Ipswich model but leaving out the Clarinet unit, thus making it a 3c/7 model, and the illuminated surround was of the "Pillar and Vase" type.

Two more small cinemas were opened in March. The first of these, the Ritz, Brighouse, was designed by J.H.Freer of the firm G.H.Haig & Co. of Huddersfield working with Union Cinemas' construction department. Situated at the junction of Bonegate Road and Bradford Road, the frontage was of Yorkshire stone, with the entrance facade in faience and white cement. There was an ornamental rock garden in front of the main entrance, along with a car park for 100 vehicles. The auditorium had seating for 986 patrons and the colour scheme blended varying shades of orange and green; a feature of the side walls took the form of shallow pilasters finished in blue and silver. Simplex projectors and the B.T.H. Sound System formed the principal equipment in the projection room. Chambers were provided for an organ, but no organ was installed. Today, however, they house the 3-manual 8-unit Wurlitzer originally installed new at the Gaumont, Oldham, later to be acquired by the Cinema Organ Society and installed in the Trinity Arts Centre in Pudsey.

The second small cinema was opened on 29 March at Felixstowe and was designed by Robert Cromie in conjunction with E.F.Tulley. The facade was in local red sand-faced bricks with white stone dressings and a notable feature was the fine window over the entrance doors. The vestibule was decorated with ornamental mirrors - a typical feature of many of the new cinemas built by the Company - and the auditorium colour scheme was in pink and bronze. There were seats for 950 patrons. As at Brighouse, Simplex projectors and the B.T.H. sound apparatus were employed.

Around this time, a number of organs installed in cinemas which had been acquired by Union Cinemas were being reopened after rebuilding and in certain cases enlargement as a result of inspection by Harold Ramsay following his arrival on the scene. One of these, at the Rivoli, Southend, has already been mentioned. Others to be so treated included the following:

The Adelphi, Slough.

The Christie 3-manual 8-unit organ was rebuilt by Compton with the addition of a Melotone unit. The console casework was changed, the new design having a more than passing resemblance to that employed by Granada for their later Wurlitzers, believed to have been designed by James Morrison, the house architect of that company. The renovated organ was opened by Alex Taylor on 4 January. Rather interestingly, the next organist to appear, a fortnight later, was A.A.Gregory, a classical musician and local borough councillor who had been the last resident at the Regal, Kingston, before the arrival there of Harold Ramsay. He had continued to make occasional appearances at Kingston and at other Union houses in the southern area.

The Regal, Beckenham.

Originally a Wurlitzer Model "F" organ of 2 manuals and 8 units, this was rebuilt by the Wurlitzer London Factory as a 3-manual instrument with grand piano attachment and a "Rainbow" illuminated surround to the console which was of course repainted in gold and fitted with the new type of music desk. Prior to the rebuild it had been featured only occasionally during 1936 with isolated visits from Alex Taylor, Jack Courtnay, Rudy Lewis, Gordon Banner and Phil Park. Stage shows were also presented from time to time and it is likely that there would have been organ accompaniment when no band had been booked to appear. The rebuilt organ was opened by Harold Ramsay on 25 January. He stayed for a second week and was followed by Sidney Torch for the next three weeks, after which Robinson Cleaver appeared for one week, then going to Oxford for the next and returning again the week after that! Clearly, considerable importance was attached to this particular instrument. Subsequent appearances were made by several other organists until Jack Dowle arrived as resident organist from week commencing 31 May.

The Regal, Altrincham.

Here, the unusual stopkey layout on the console of the Compton organ, in which all the speaking stops derived from certain units were placed together in "families" and the Solo or third manual was split as between treble and bass so as to permit two types of registration on that manual at the same time, was abolished. This layout had been specified originally by the organist Norman Cocker, who was also assistant organist at Manchester Cathedral and a distinguished composer of organ music. Harold Ramsay took the decision to replace it with a conventional layout, chiefly to simplify matters for visiting organists touring the circuit. In any event, as previously mentioned, standardisation of console layouts had been adopted as an ongoing policy in the cinema organ world. Ramsay himself reopened the organ on 8 February, on which occasion the organ misbehaved itself by blowing a fuse and refusing to play after about five minutes into the programme; the great man continued on piano, accompanying a vocalist, while things were put right and he was able to continue at the organ!

The Kingsway, Levenshulme.

The organ at this cinema was originally a product of the Manchester firm of organ-builders Jardine & Co. Ltd. and had 3 Manuals and 10 units, together with a "Rex Gloria" illuminated surround - Jardines claimed to be first in the field with illuminated consoles. Harold Ramsay evidently felt that the time had come for an overhaul and entrusted the work to Compton. The illuminated console surround was removed and replaced by wooden casework similar to that supplied to the Adelphi, Slough.

Again, Harold Ramsay himself appeared for the reopening on 15 February. It was evidently a busy week for him as he was also billed to play at the Broadway, Eccles, where as far as I can discover no alterations were made to the 1932-vintage Christie organ at that cinema.

On 2 March the BBC broadcast a variety show entitled "Radio Round-up" from the stage of the Regal, Kingston, "roping in" the very popular top of the bill artistes Renée Houston and Donald Stewart, specialising in witty songs and clever cross-talk, Clapham & Dwyer in "another spot of bother" and several other acts. For the first time, Harold Ramsay, Sidney Torch and Robinson Cleaver appeared together in the same programme, alternating between the organ and two grand pianos, and "The Regal Variety Orchestra" was also included, together with the audience of the Regal Cinema. Continuity and special lyrics were by Phil Park. The broadcast went out on the London Regional wavelength

74

of the BBC, starting at 9.00 pm and lasting forty minutes. The title "Round-up" was inspired by the rounding-up of stock by cowboys on horseback and in this case it was the variety artistes who were being "rounded up" or "roped in." The scene on stage was of a ranch setting, with a handful of "cowboys" (stage hands?) dotted around to add to the effect. Interestingly, the local press and Union's own publicity gave the show the title "Radio Rodeo" and this would be adopted by Radio Times for subsequent editions. I wonder if it was not used for the first broadcast because someone at the BBC decided that listeners would not be familiar with the word "Rodeo"?

The broadcast was an immense success, not simply because it was quite unusual for the BBC to broadcast variety shows in mid-week, but because of the sheer novelty of the presentation. Apparently the switchboard at Broadcasting House was inundated with calls asking for more: thus was initiated the famous series of broadcasts which recommenced in May and continued monthly right through to October. As we shall see, a great many of the leading stars of the variety stage appeared in the show during this period.

Cinema organ broadcasts from the Ritz, Belfast, continued during this period and were as follows:

Date	Time	Organist	Wavelength
9.1.37	11.00	Cecil Chadwick	National
16.1.37	9.00	" "	Northern Ireland
23.1.37	11.00	" "	National
23.1.37	9.00	" "	Northern Ireland
25.1.37	7.30	" "	" "
5.2.37	10.45	Robinson Cleaver	Regional
12.2.37	9.00	" "	Northern Ireland
19.2.37	10.45	" "	Regional
25.2.37	8.30	" "	Northern Ireland
5.3.37	10.45	Frank Matthew	Regional
10.3.37	6.40	" "	Northern Ireland
19.3.37	10.45	Elaine Bair	Regional
25.3.37	6.30	Joseph Seal	Northern Ireland

In point of fact, the organists in the above list were those actually appearing at the Ritz during the weeks in which they broadcast. Frank Matthew, like Alex Taylor, had broadcast fairly regularly in the late 1920's and it was good to see him back on the air again. For Elaine

Bair it was almost a "first": two days earlier, on 17 March, the Northern Ireland page in Radio Times announced "Variety from the Ritz Cinema, Belfast" at 8.15. No other details were given, but in the house magazine it was described as "Union Cinemas Radio Stage Show" featuring comedians Clapham & Dwyer, tenor Fred Hudson "and other famous acts", plus "At the organ - Miss Elaine Bair." It is interesting to note that the transmissions listed above were divided between mornings on the National or Regional programmes and evenings on the Northern Ireland Region only. Joseph Seal was to become resident at Belfast, but not yet: Neville Meale, Andrée Conti and Jack Dowle appeared for two weeks each after Seal's initial four-week run, but did not broadcast while they were there. Originally, it had been the intention that Cecil Chadwick should take up the position of resident organist, but the plan was changed and he returned to the Capitol, Didsbury, as his base theatre, resuming broadcasts from there and making occasional appearances at other Union houses in the Northern Area. Sidney Torch gave an isolated broadcast from the Capitol, Didsbury, on 18 January.

Harold Ramsay continued his organ broadcasts from the Regal, Kingston. He also made records there, as he was under contract to the Parlophone label, and eventually a total of ten solo 10" 78's plus one more which featured community singing by the Regal audience, accompanied on the organ. Community singing was always on the menu wherever Ramsay appeared, and at Kingston as already noted the cowboy song "Home on the Range" became almost an anthem at that cinema.

Robinson Cleaver also continued his broadcasts from the Regal, Bexley Heath. He, too, had a recording contract with Parlophone and a total of twelve 10" 78's were issued. In addition, he made one for Octacross, a label offering organ recordings for trade use only.

From time to time, more organists were added to the team to keep pace with the expansion programme. Barry Bretonner, a Yorkshireman by birth but who lived in Australia from the age of twelve, returned to England on honeymoon with his New Zealand bride whom he had met whilst touring that country. In Australia and New Zealand he became famous as a cinema organist, touring extensively as "The Wonder Boy Organist" and broadcasting regularly. He became a Fellow of Trinity College, London, at the age of 24 years, the youngest Australian to gain that honour. The story goes that back in Yorkshire he paid a visit to the Ritz, Huddersfield, in a week when the organ was not being featured, saw the console down in the orchestra pit and decided to introduce himself to the Manager with a view to trying the organ out. He was rapidly taken on board by Union Cinemas, becoming resident at Huddersfield from 22 March and making occasional sorties to other cinemas in the Northern Area, including Scunthorpe and Greater Manchester.

Another experienced organist was Hubert Selby, previously with Gaumont-British. Some sources state that he was with Union Cinemas in 1936-37, but the earliest advertised appearance on tour I have been able to trace was for the week commencing 22 March at the Ritz, Oxford, although he had by then spent some time at the Capitol, Didsbury. He toured the circuit more widely, but mainly in the South.

"The attractive lady organist" Beverley Hall was featured at the Ritz, Oxford, the week after Hubert Selby's appearance there, subsequently being billed at Scunthorpe and Barnsley. I can find no further mention of her after week commencing 12 July.

Harold Ramsay was making frequent broadcasts from the Regal, Kingston, quite often on a Saturday afternoon when there would be audience participation in the form of community singing. On Saturday 6 March his broadcast at 2.30 pm was advertised in Radio Times as coming from the Regal, Kingston, but the announcer introducing the programme stated that it was coming from the Union, Kingston; the name actually changed that weekend.

News emerged in March of more new cinemas which in the event did not materialise. One concerned a Ritz to be built in Otley, where Union Cinemas offered £3,000 for a site; it appears, however, that nothing came of it. In Heywood plans were approved for a Ritz cinema to be erected at the corner of Bridge Street and St. James' Street, and in Lancaster it was said that work would start shortly in Dalton Square.

In April it was announced that the Construction Department of the Company had moved to Jubilee House, 207-213 Oxford Street, London W.1., occupying the 4th floor of that building. It was referred to in the announcement as Cinema Developments Ltd., a subsidiary about which more would be heard at a later date.

CHAPTER SEVEN

CORONATION YEAR

Further important openings of new cinemas took place during the next few months of 1937. In addition, promotional activity increased considerably and so did the number of broadcasts. It could fairly be said that the best days of Union Cinemas had arrived.

The "Grand Gala Opening" of the Ritz, Woking, took place at 7.45 pm on 12 April, the opening ceremony itself being performed by Godfrey Nicholson M.P., and once again a distinguished company of guests was present. There was a stage show and Harold Ramsay was at the organ. The main feature film was "The Texas Rangers" starring Fred MacMurray, Jack Oakie and Jean Parker.

This opening marked the official debut of the Union Cinemas Ladies Accordion Band, fronted by Gypsy Nina - "Accordionist and Singer from the Great White Way." It was stated that there had been no less than 433 auditions in all parts of the country, from which 18 players were finally selected to form the band. Certainly the result was extremely successful, players, costumes and music adding up to a most attractive stage presentation. Other acts included Stanford & McNaughton "The Wise Jesters", and O'Shea & Joan "The Original Staircase Dancers - Stepping it Out."

The Ritz was designed by architects Verity & Beverley in consultation with E.F.Tulley and was situated on a prominent site in Chobham Road near the town centre. An interesting feature was the curved entrance, with a double line of glass doors to provide a draught lobby before entering the main vestibule leading to the stalls and wide staircases up to the balcony and café-restaurant. The decorative scheme was in graded tones of terra-cotta, peach and gold, much in line with other cinemas recently opened by the Company. The use of ornamental mirrors and handsome light fittings followed the same trend. The auditorium seated 1,518 patrons, whilst the stage was of generous size, being fully equipped for the presentation of the variety acts which formed such an important part of Union Cinemas' programming policy. The projection room contained the latest equipment including the latest Western Electric "Mirrophonic" sound system.

The Compton organ was of a new type of 3-manual 6-unit instrument with Melotone specially developed for Union Cinemas. Whilst in outline the specification resembled that of the standard Compton 3-manual 6-unit model of which so many examples were built, to some extent it represented an enlarged version of the 2-manual 4-unit model introduced at the Ritz cinemas at Horsham and Penzance. Harold Ramsay was clearly impressed with this model and wished the standard 6-unit model to be upgraded on similar lines. The Tibia was to be of wood instead of the metal rank generally used by Compton. The Gamba was replaced by a two-rank Strings unit of the type more usually found in larger Compton organs. The Flute unit was retained, as was the Tromba. Interestingly, for a second reed a Krumet unit was specified. The sixth unit was a Diaphonic Diapason. The swell shutter system chosen was similar to that used in the 4-unit model. It is understood that the new model was substantially more expensive than the standard model. In later years many organists declared it the more satisfying to play. The "Pillar and Vase" style of illuminated console surround was fitted. Robinson Cleaver was the featured organist for the second week and Sidney Torch for the third.

One week later, on 19 April, the Regal in Cowley Road, Oxford, was opened. It was the second new Union Cinema to be built in the town, the first of course having been the Ritz. The Opening Ceremony on this occasion was performed by the Deputy Mayor. There was a stage show which included Zigano's Anglo-French Accordion Band - "Rhythm! Melody! Novelty! Surprise!" - Stanford & McNaughton and other acts, and Sidney Torch was at the organ.

Like the Ritz, this cinema was another to be designed by Robert Cromie, with a seating capacity of 1,674, slightly more than that of the earlier cinema in George Street. The construction, decoration and equipment were fairly typical of the new cinemas being built by the Company, the foyer being particularly noteworthy. The Compton organ again seemed to owe something to the 2-manual 4-unit model, this time being enlarged to include a third (coupler) manual and an additional pipe unit, a Diaphonic Diapason, plus of course the usual Melotone attachment. However, the Tromba was replaced by the more usual Tuba unit. The by now standard "Pillar and Vase" illuminated console surround was fitted.

With the new building programme in full swing the "Union look" was becoming ever more distinctive. Architecture, interior decoration, lighting, carpeting, upholstery, stage drapes and so on all pointed to a certain similarity of style. The exclusive "Pillar and Vase" illuminated console surround mentioned above was typical of this trend. Another element contributing to the "look" was to be found in the uniforms worn by front of house staff. (The popular term used today is "corporate clothing"). Those for the men were in a fairly dark olive green with facings in light green and silver trim. For the ladies the main colour was rose pink with dove grey facings and gold lace trim. The uniforms were supplied by the leading firm of Edward Harold (Uniforms) Ltd. whose head office was situated in Wardour Street in London's West End.

Sidney Torch remained at the organ for the opening week. He was followed by Alex Taylor for the next three weeks, Pierson Webber for three more and then Harold Ramsay for one. Later, appearances were made by Rudy Lewis and Robinson Cleaver, but flooding problems in the under-stage chambers led to the organ being removed for use elsewhere.

Plans were announced in April for a new Ritz Cinema to be built in Eastbourne at the corner of Tideswell Road and Junction Road to the designs of W.T.Benslyn. Planning permission was granted by the Eastbourne Corporation on the understanding that the cinema would be completed within two years, but in the event this project did not come to fruition. It may seem a little odd that it was mooted in the first place, considering that Union Cinemas had already acquired the notable Luxor in the town and were enjoying satisfactory returns there.

Cinema organ broadcasts by the Company's leading organists seemed to be on the increase: Harold Ramsay himself gave four during the month, all from the Union, Kingston, one of them - to the Empire - on 27 April, commencing at 3.45 am ! Robinson Cleaver gave three from the Regal, Bexley Heath, including another Empire transmission - this one commencing at 4.10 am. on 21 April. Joseph Seal also gave three broadcasts, these of course being from the Ritz, Belfast, and Sidney Torch gave what I believe to have been the first of his broadcasts from the Union, Kingston, on 23 April.

As previously mentioned, the belated Opening of the Wurlitzer organ at the Ritz, Barnsley, took place on 26 April, the Deputy Mayor of the town officiating and Robinson Cleaver being the featured organist for the occasion. He remained for the first week and was followed by Pierson Webber, Elaine Bair, Barry Bretonner (two weeks) and Edward Farley. Beverley Hall took up a short residency week commencing 14 June.

Following the success of the initial "Radio Round-Up" broadcast in March which I have already described, the first of the monthly series of similar transmissions went out on 6 May at 7.50 pm. A number of changes were made to the format, including the adoption of "Radio Rodeo" as the title of the show. A special signature tune opened the programme: the "Rodeo March" composed by Harold Ramsay, with words by Phil Park, and sung by the cinema audience. The Regal Variety Orchestra was dropped and the musical accompaniment was provided by the organ, two pianos and percussion. A really strong bill was headed by the great comedian George Robey; also included were Clapham & Dwyer, the Carlyle Cousins, Randolph Sutton - billed as "Britain's Premier Light Comedian", Stanford & McNaughton, Gypsy Nina and the Ladies Accordion Band and the Gordon Ray Radiolympia Girls. Sidney Torch, Robinson Cleaver and Phil Park all took part, together with Harold Ramsay himself who compéred the show which was produced by Leon Pollock, the Company's Manager of Stage Production.

During the week, an abridged version of the show was staged daily at each performance, leaving out the "top of the bill" artiste and one or two other items; this still amounted to a more than usually lavish presentation. It was not long before the decision was taken to commence touring succeeding editions of the "Radio Rodeo" show, not only around the Union circuit but the Paramount one as well. When one of the leading organists was not available to accompany the show, Peggy Weber filled the role. At Paramount the show reverted to its original name "Radio Round-up" and was accompanied by one of their own organists - for example, at the Paramount, Manchester, for the week commencing 24 May the organist was the resident at that cinema, Henry Croudson.

The "Grand Coronation Gala Opening" of the Ritz, Aldershot, took place on Thursday 13 May at 2.30. pm., the Mayor and Mayoress officiating. Virtually all of the previous openings had been on a Monday, with one or two on a Saturday evening, but because of the Coronation of King George VI on 12 May an exception was made in this case and the programme ran for four days only, including the Sunday. The stage show featured Gypsy Nina and the Ladies Accordion Band and Harold Ramsay - "acknowledged the world's leading broadcasting organist" - was at the organ. On the previous Monday there had been an advertisement in the Daily Mirror announcing the opening and stating that the Coronation Speech of H.M. the King would be relayed at all Union Cinemas throughout the country.

The Ritz, Aldershot, was built to the plans of Verity & Beverley and seated 1,747 patrons. It was described as a sister cinema to the Ritz, Woking, and certainly there were some similarities. Its decoration and equipment followed closely that of other cinemas recently opened by the Company, with the familiar auditorium colour scheme of terra cotta, peach and gold. The large stage was up to the usual standard for the presentation of variety acts.

The organ was a Wurlitzer of 3 manuals and 7 units with "phantom" grand piano attachment mounted on the stage and was almost identical to that of the Ritz, Barnsley, incorporating just a few minor modifications The "Pillar and Vase" illuminated surround was fitted to the console. In the first full week after the opening, Robinson Cleaver was the organist and the stage show was supplied by Billy Cotton and his Band. In due course it became fairly common for the organist to double between Aldershot and Woking and Sidney Torch was the first to do this, appearing at both cinemas for the week commencing 7 June.

Whilst on the subject of organists, it is interesting to note that the Ritz, Aldershot, was situated on an island site adjoining the existing Empire Cinema: this possessed a small 2-manual Compton organ and for the months of April to July some extra competition for the Ritz was provided by featuring a number of guest organists. These included Andrew Fenner (from the Regal, Wimbledon), John Howlett (Regal, Hull), Guy Hindell (Astoria and Ritz, Southend), James Peters (Plaza and Regal, Southampton), Jack Courtnay (Astoria, Folkestone), Gerald Masters (Regal, Margate) and Jack Helyer (Ritz, Nottingham) who made no less than three visits during this period.

Another opening took place on 31 May: the Ritz, Wokingham, this being quite a small cinema seating only 716 patrons. E. Norman Bailey was the architect, well-known for his work elsewhere, notably the Regal, Uxbridge. The exterior was in red brick with stone dressings and an interesting feature was a corner tower with fins carrying the cinema's name; the entrance being situated at the opposite corner. The

The next "Radio Rodeo" broadcast from the Union, Kingston, was on Wednesday 14 July at 8.20 pm and once again there was an impressive line-up of artistes. Top of the bill were the celebrated Flanagan and Allen, together with comedians Tommy Handley and Ronald Frankeau presenting another episode from the somewhat confused lives of "Mr Murgatroyd and Mr Winterbottom", Rudy Starita, Steffani and his 21 Silver Songsters, Cecil Johnson and Angela Parselles. Messrs. Ramsay, Torch, Cleaver and Park were on hand as usual to provide the musical accompaniment. Harold Ramsay compéred the show, Phil Park wrote the continuity and special lyrics and Leon Pollock was the producer.

An advertisement in the Daily Mirror on the Monday stated that advance bookings for the broadcast already exceeded 2,000 - such was the interest in being present on the evening itself. It had become quite usual for large crowds to gather outside the cinema earlier in the evening - perhaps hoping to gain entry to the cinema, or at least to catch a glimpse of the artistes arriving for the show.

At the beginning of July Mr Adams, previously Assistant Director of Theatre Construction, was appointed Theatre Controller. In this capacity he subsequently appeared on stage at most of the openings of new cinemas. I have been unable to ascertain the movements of Leslie Holderness, the previous Theatre Controller, but assume that he returned to duties within the Paramount Group.

At the same time, Leslie H.Kemp F.I.A.A. was appointed Director of Theatre Construction in succession to J.H.Lundy. An article by Mr Lundy entitled "The Architect and the Showman" appeared in the trade press concurrently with the announcements referred to above.

The advertisement in the "Daily Mirror" on 12 July also announced that Dudley Savage, "The Cornish Wonder Boy Organist", would be appearing all that week at the Ritz, Aldershot, and should not be missed. With him were three other talented youngsters: Marjorie Dale (14) and Cecil Hardy (16), both singers, and Evelyn Pearson (20), a violinist. This small group was actually touring the circuit at the time and appeared to be well received by audiences. Marjorie Dale would later be engaged as a voclaist with the Billy cotton Band.

Dudley Savage, as mentioned earlier, had met Harold Ramsay at Penzance when the latter visited the town to open the Ritz there on 27 July 1936. He underwent training at Kingston whilst acting as house organist at Horsham, then making his first public appearance at

Penzance on 11 January 1937 and his Kingston debut on 1 February. After two weeks at Kingston, he set off on tour - starting at the Regal, Yarmouth, on 15 February. He quickly established himself as a very popular performer, laying the foundations for what was to become a distinguished career as a concert organist in the years to follow.

On Thursday 22 July the first of two more major Openings took place: this was at the Ritz, Nuneaton. As usual the Mayor of the town officiated, accompanied by the Mayoress. In addition to the film programme, Macari and his Dutch Accordion Serenaders formed the spectacular stage show and Alex Taylor was at the organ.

Situated on the corner of Abbey Street and Newtown Road, this cinema was built to plans drawn up by Verity & Beverley. The elevation was in brick and stone and was on simple though modern lines. There were double lines of entrance doors to provide a draught lobby, leading to a spacious vestibule, decorative features including ornamental mirrors and stylish illumination. The colour scheme in the 1,674-seat auditorium was carried out once again in graded tones of terra cotta, peach and gold. The proscenium arch included a decorated grille opening at the top behind which were located the organ chambers, with similar sets of grilles in illuminated recesses with fabric curtains on either side. The large stage was fully equipped for the presentation of variety entertainment, with ample dressing room accommodation close at hand. The projection room was likewise lavishly equipped, with Western Electric "Mirrophonic" sound system and Simplex projectors, non-synchronous attachment and high-intensity arcs.

The organ was a Compton 3-manual with 6 pipe units and Melotone, being in fact another of the special models developed for Union Cinemas first seen at the Ritz, Woking. Alex Taylor continued to appear for the remainder of the opening week and for the two weeks which followed, Barry Bretonner arriving for the next two weeks. Later, Gordon Banner and Neville Meale made a number of appearances, with Dudley Savage there for the week commencing 18 October.

The second major Opening was at the Ritz, Cleethorpes, on Saturday 31 July, the Mayor of Cleethorpes officiating, in the presence of the Mayoress and also of the Mayor and Mayoress of Grimsby. Actually, it was interesting to note that in the local press the cinema was referred to as the Ritz, Grimsby, being situated in Grimsby Road near the town football ground and on the main trolley-bus route between the two towns. The opening ceremony itself included a fanfare of trumpets and there was an introductory speech by Herbert Stevens, Manager of the Ritz, Huddersfield, and formerly well-known as a theatre manager in the locality. He stated that after joining Union Cinemas he had suggested to Frederick Bernhard that the Company should build a new cinema in the district and was told to go ahead and find a suitable site. Others present at the opening included Sir Walter Womersley MP and Lady Womersley, J.H.Lundy and E.R.Adams of Union Cinemas and M.J.Sharp who had been appointed resident manager of the new cinema. Robinson Cleaver was at the organ and he also introduced the "In Town Tonight" feature in which local personalities were interviewed, including among others one of the first tram drivers in Grimsby and the coach from the Grimsby Town Football Club.

The Ritz was designed by Robert Cromie, the facade being in dull red brick with white stone dressings. There were double rows of entrance doors to provide a draught lobby, with the vestibule enhanced by the artistic use of ornamental mirrors and light fittings. The auditorium was somewhat smaller than that at Nuneaton, seating 1,429 patrons, and was finished in shades of terra cotta, peach and gold, with an elaborate grille feature rising from one side, carried right across the ceiling and down the other side. No doubt because of this, the actual proscenium opening was unusually simple. The stage was large and well equipped, together with ample dressing room accommodation for visiting artistes. Powerful modern projectors, "Mirrophonic" sound apparatus with non-synchronous attachment and high-intensity arcs were provided in the projection room.

The organ was the third of the special Compton 3-manual 6-unit plus Melotone instruments to be supplied to Union Cinemas. Robinson Cleaver played for the week after the opening, being followed on 9 August by Alex Taylor and a stage show which included Randolph Sutton and Fields & Rossini. Tommy Fields was Gracie Fields' brother and with his partner was another "regular" on the circuit; as well as comedy, they were accomplished musicians, Fields playing the violin and Rossini the accordion. In due course Harold Ramsay appeared at Cleethorpes for the week commencing 30 August, but perhaps rather strangely he never appeared at Nuneaton during the Union days. In time the Nuneaton organ came to be recognised as the best of the "Ramsay Specials" and today its sounds can still be appreciated in the Catholic Church of St. John Vianney in the East London suburb of Clayhall where concerts continue to be held regularly.

It was the usual practice for local newspapers to concentrate advertisements and editorials dealing with the week's entertainments on one page and by and large the latter consisted of straightforward accounts of forthcoming films and shows. In the case of Cleethorpes, however, the weekly review was supplied by someone called "The Stroller" who evidently felt it desirable to offer criticisms of items already seen. The organists were fair game in this respect. Of Alex Taylor it was said "Alex Taylor produces a tremendous volume of sound and one occasionally wishes for a more judicious application of the soft pedal." There was a qualified write-up on Harold Ramsay's performance, finishing with the words "The best and most important thing about him is that he gives his audiences a great deal of pleasure." As for Paul Gomez and Barrie Moore, who had a three-week run after Ramsay, the remark was "The performance is competent but undistinguished." One can only speculate as to whether the newspaper's editor received complaints from Union Cinemas or from the artistes themselves, as such comments apparently ceased thereafter.

As well as the July "Radio Rodeo" broadcast, solo organ broadcasts continued during the month. These included four by Joseph Seal from Belfast, two by Harold Ramsay from Kingston, one of these being to the Empire at 6.15 am on 13 July, two by Robinson Cleaver from Bexley Heath, one by Sidney Torch from Kingston to the Empire at 3.00 am on 22 July and one by Cecil Chadwick from Didsbury. Of course all broadcasts in those days went out "live" and it is interesting to note that transmissions to the Empire took place at quite ungodly hours! The organists had to have strong constitutions, playing their normal interludes during the day as well as endeavouring to do justice to live broadcasts in the early hours.

On 30 July the Ritz, Tonbridge, was declared open by the Vice-Chairman of the Tonbridge Urban District Council. On the stage with him were E.R.Adams, representing the Union Cinemas Management, Mr Beverley, representing the architects Verity & Beverley, and Alan Colston, the resident manager of the cinema.

The cinema was situated in a very short street known as the Botany and had a facade in brick with stone dressings. It had a double row of glass entrance doors to provide a draught lobby leading into the spacious vestibule. The interior of the 1,250-seat auditorium included a balcony and was decorated in the by now standard colour scheme of terra cotta, peach and gold. The sound and projection equipment was also of standard specification and there was a small stage but no organ. Smaller cinemas than this on the circuit possessed an organ and it may be that budget considerations ruled it out in this instance.

Another small cinema was opened on 2 August: the Ritz, Erith, a short distance to the north of Bexley Heath. This was not in fact a new cinema, but a two-month reconstruction of an existing cinema, the Picture House, built in 1928 and taken over as part of the Sidney Bacon circuit in 1935. It was a comparatively small house, with the auditorium arranged on one floor only. The reconstruction really amounted to a general redecoration and refurbishment, with one or two embellishments inside and out to give the place more of a "Union" look.

A trade announcement on 5 August stated that a further twelve existing cinemas were being added to the circuit, as follows:

Perrymount, Haywards Heath	Albert Hall, Swansea
Broadway, " "	Carlton, "
Palace, Leyland	Picture House, "
Regent, "	Knowle Hall, Neath
Palace, Londonderry	Windsor, "
Rialto, "	Palace, Ammanford

On the whole, this could be considered a fairly nondescript batch of cinemas and the wisdom of acquiring them could perhaps be queried. It was clear that the Company was eager to increase the size of the circuit generally and that the stated policy was to obtain control of all the cinemas in a given town in order to strengthen its bargaining power in the matter of film rentals. Even so, given that substantial progress had been made to date in the development of the circuit, the fact remained that a large proportion of the houses were of questionable quality. With the programme of new construction proceeding at quite a satisfactory rate, perhaps after all it would have made more sense to close some of the older houses that had been acquired earlier. By this time, however, the Company's publicity department was boasting that the number of cinemas it operated would probably pass the 300 mark by the end of the year, so closures were not to be encouraged! Exaggeration certainly ruled the day: in reality there was nothing like this number.

At Haywards Heath, hoardings at a site in South Road announced that a new Ritz cinema was to be built there, complete with stage and organ. The trade press also referred to this, but stated that no architect had yet been appointed. Nothing further seems to have occurred and in retrospect it has even been suggested that the whole episode might have been an elaborate ploy to dissuade Odeon from building in the town.

The same press release dealing with the acquisitions mentioned above also stated that sites for new cinemas had also been identified at Grays, Crawley, Sandwich, Faversham, Strood, Sevenoaks, Newhaven, Seaford and Havant. It was announced that Crawley and Strood were to be ready for opening by Christmas but it appears that events in due course overtook these plans and nothing came to fruition in Union Cinemas' time. The same could be said for Alton, where Leslie Kemp was said to be drawing up plans for another new cinema; again, nothing came of it.

The August edition of "Radio Rodeo" was broadcast from the Union, Kingston, on Wednesday 11 August at 8.35 pm . Top of the bill was the famous star of stage and screen Cicely Courtneidge, supported by the eccentric comedian Claude Dampier assisted by Billy Carlyle, together with Billy Costello, who provided the voice of Popeye the Sailor in the popular "Popeye" cartoon films, The Four Aces, Rusty & Shine and the four regular organists including Harold Ramsay who also acted as compére. As usual, the show was produced by Leon Pollock.

An advertisement which appeared in the Daily Mirror on the previous Monday was headed "Scramble to see Broadcast of "Radio Rodeo" from the Union Cinema", referring to "amazing scenes witnessed outside the cinema" and making much of the large numbers of people who had been unable to gain admission for the July edition. This advertisement went on to mention that Andrée Conti would be broadcasting from the Union, Kingston, in the near future and drew attention to the fact that she was not only an organist but also played the piano and xylophone, usually in conjunction with an organ accompaniment recorded by herself, and possessed a fine contralto voice. It is my belief that this broadcast did not actually take place.

The next important Opening was on 23 August: the Ritz, Warrington. As usual, the Mayor officiated at the ceremony, accompanied by the Mayoress, and Leslie H Kemp and E.R.Adams were also present on stage with their wives. The General Manager appointed to this cinema was Gerald James who not only introduced the guests but also acted as compére for the "In Town Tonight" feature: this included members of the Warrington Rugby Football Club and a number of well-known local personalities. The stage show featured Macari and his Dutch Accordion Serenaders, Tommy Fields and Rossini, and O'Shea and Joan - "The Original Staircase Dancers." Alex Taylor presided at the organ and later the local press reported in typical vein "The sounds it can produce brought exclamations of amazement from the audience!" In addition, the programme included two feature films: "Without Orders" starring Robert Armstrong and Sally Eilers, and "I Promise to Pay" with Chester Morris and Leo Carillo. In his speech at the opening E.R.Adams said that only the best was good enough for Warrington and the aim of the company was to ensure success by providing healthy, clean and good entertainment in both films and variety.

The Ritz was situated in Barbauld Street and presented a somewhat different "look" from others recently opened, the architect on this occasion being J.Owen Bond. It seated 1,928 patrons and maintained the same high standards of decoration and equipment as other new Union houses. The organ was the fourth in the series of Ramsay "Specials" to be built by Compton with 3 manuals and 6 units plus Melotone.

In addition to the "Radio Rodeo" variety show from Kingston, there was another good crop of organ broadcasts during the month. Once again, Joseph Seal gave four from Belfast and Harold Ramsay and Sidney Torch each gave two from Kingston. Robinson Cleaver, however, only gave one from Bexley Heath.

It is perhaps noteworthy that in planning the tour rosters for the various organists employed by the Company, special efforts were made to ensure that the top three (Harold Ramsay, Sidney Torch and Robinson Cleaver) all made appearances at cinemas at or near seaside resorts. Thus in the months of July and August Ramsay appeared twice each at Eastbourne, St. Leonards and Penzance, and once each at Yarmouth, Southend and Cleethorpes. Torch appeared at Yarmouth, Southend and Eastbourne, and Cleaver at Southend, Eastbourne, St. Leonards, Cleethorpes and Penzance. The Daily Mirror advertisement on 9 August referred to above mentioned that Robinson Cleaver was at St. Leonards all that week and went on to say "This is an artiste you must not fail to hear!" Presumably he had to miss his evening interlude on the Wednesday, as he had to be at Kingston for the "Radio Rodeo" broadcast; I know this to be true because I attended that broadcast and saw him there!

The distinguished organist Cecil Chadwick who had joined the Company at the Capitol, Didsbury, in September 1936, gave his last performance on 28 August and left to take up another appointment elsewhere. During his months with Union, he had spent virtually the whole of his time at Didsbury, from where he broadcast on several occasions, but also toured the cinemas located in the Northern Area. Interestingly, the next broadcast to be given from Didsbury was by

Barry Bretonner on 3 September. It would appear that this was the only broadcast to be given by him, so it is quite possible that this date had already been booked by the BBC for Cecil Chadwick and that Bretonner replaced him at relatively short notice (though it was his name which was published in Radio Times).

In September a press release announced the setting up of four Trust Companies, private and unlimited, with David Bernhard, Chairman of Union Cinemas, as Chairman and Governing Director, together with two other directors. These companies were:

> Actor Investment Trust Co.
> Bisham Investment Trust Co.
> Braemour Investment Trust Co.
> Windmill Investment Trust Co.

The purpose of each of these companies was to carry on the business of a general investment trust company. Very few, if any, business transactions could have taken place, however, as on 15 September Mr Bernhard died at the age of 76 years.

David Bernhard's funeral service took place at Shirley Parish Church, with cremation following later at the Croydon Crematorium. The service at the church was conducted by the Vicar, the Rev.G.C.Rawlins, with Harold Ramsay at the organ, and the large congregation packed the building to the doors. Some 250 wreaths and floral tributes were sent. The Bernhard Family were of course present in strength, including not only Frederick Bernhard and his wife but also his brothers Herbert and Frank. Directors and Senior Management members of Union Cinemas were also there in force, including L.J.Clements, L.H.Kemp, J.H.Lundy, J.Jarratt, E.R.Adams, Montague Lyon, Leon Pollock, V.Hayes-Jones, Captain H.W.Rifkin and many more. The Royal Philatelic Society was represented by three officials, David Bernhard having been an active Member and owning one of the most important stamp collections in existence; indeed, he had been on good terms with the late King George V and visited Buckingham Palace regularly to "talk stamps" with the King, himself a keen collector.

The death of David Bernhard not surprisingly affected the Company's share prices: the Ordinary Shares which had stood at 5s.6d. earlier in the year dropped as low as 7½d. before recovering to 1s.9d. and the Chairman's holding had been 1,103,652 shares, in addition to his holdings of First and Second Preference shares, the prices of which were also affected to a lesser degree. In the trade press, however, it was announced that important financial arrangements had been made and that fears of a large block of shares coming onto the market were unfounded. During the weeks that followed, there was some further recovery in the prices whilst news of developments to come was anxiously awaited by shareholders.

The next edition of the "Radio Rodeo" Show was broadcast from the Union, Kingston, on Thursday 16 September at 8.00 pm. No less a star than Gracie Fields topped the bill on this occasion, supported by the famous child impersonator Harry Hemsley, Bower & Rutherford (The Joy Bombs in New Explosions), Leslie Strange (the Political Jester), tenor Fred Hudson and the usual line-up of organists. Once again, the broadcast was a great success.

An amusing story was related by Union organist Peggy Weber: it appeared that Gracie Fields made her entry on stage during the show in a horse-drawn carriage and that when she went to step down she found that the door would not open! Somehow it had been locked and for a few moments she struggled with it before Harold Ramsay, realising what had happened, rushed forward and succeeded in opening the door from the outside. Gracie made a characteristic "ad lib" remark about getting stuck! All this during a live broadcast!

Another new cinema was opened on 27 September, being the Union, Dunstable, designed by Leslie H.Kemp and having 1432 seats. It was built next door to the Palace, an older and considerably smaller cinema also owned by Union Cinemas; thus the company had two cinemas operating in the town, presumably to deter competitors from entering the scene.

Union Cinemas entered the commercial radio scene in August, beginning a regular weekly series of broadcasts from Radio Normandy, across the English Channel. This was done in conjunction with the International Broadcasting Company and entailed a considerable amount of ingenuity, as each programme had to be recorded - old-style gramophone fashion - on stage at the Union, Kingston, on Sunday morning, the records then being flown across to Normandy for transmission the following Sunday at 11.15 am. A special club was formed at the cinema to provide a live audience for each show. It is not quite clear when the first broadcast took place: on 8 August Radio Pictorial announced a military band for the half-hour slot commencing at 11.15, on the 15th "a surprise programme" and on the 22nd "Union Cinemas present" a show featuring Harold Ramsay, Andrée Conti, Iran Jackson and Fred Hudson. The surprise programme may have been a similar transmission. The broadcast on 29 August was announced as "Radio Parade", with the same artistes as the previous week, so it is reasonable to conclude that these were pilot broadcasts to test everything out. The first fully-fledged "Radio Parade" broadcast took place on 5 September, with the Two Leslies (Leslie Holmes and Leslie Sarony with songs at the piano, usually written by themselves), Tollefson (virtuoso accordionist) and a strong supporting bill, with Harold Ramsay himself at the organ and presenting the show. A new signature tune was needed for the show and the story goes that Ramsay composed it earlier in the summer when he was appearing at the Ritz, Penzance, rang Phil Park and hummed it to him over the phone so that he could write it down and produce a suitable lyric for it!

Harold Ramsay played the organ for the next two broadcasts and from 19 September Robinson Cleaver and Jack Dowle were featured, Ramsay appearing as compére. In due course Phil Park joined the team. In charge of the control booth at the side of the stage for each recording were two men who in later years were to become very famous broadcasters in their own right: Jack Hargreaves (for his "Out of Town" series on commercial television dealing with rural topics) and Roy Plomley (for his "Desert Island Discs" radio programmes at the BBC).

Rather curiously, in addition to the "Radio Parade" shows, another series began on Radio Normandy entitled "Around the Union Cinemas." Each programme was of fifteen minutes' duration and featured Harold Ramsay and guest artistes. The show was broadcast on Mondays, commencing 30 August, and was repeated on Wednesday and Saturday each week. As with "Radio Parade", the sponsors were Union Cinemas Ltd. themselves, suggesting that the company was promoting itself heavily - and no doubt at some considerable expense.

But this was not all. Commencing Sunday 5 September on Radio Luxembourg, Harold Ramsay and a guest artiste (on this occasion Hal Yates) were featured in another weekly series, "Peter the Planter Presents" sponsored by the makers of Lyons Green Label Tea!

Back with the BBC, apart from the broadcast by Barry Bretonner from the Capitol, Didsbury, on 3 September already mentioned, Joseph Seal and Robinson Cleaver each gave three (one of Cleaver's being an Empire broadcast starting at 1.40 am), Harold Ramsay gave two and Sidney Torch gave one.

96

CHAPTER NINE

A UNION WITH ABC

In the course of the final quarter of the year 1937 various management problems and financial difficulties began to surface. The death of the Chairman, David Bernhard, had clearly brought these matters to a head and it became increasingly clear that things could not go on as they were. I will seek to describe the sequence of events month by month in parallel with the ongoing activities of the Company.

The "Grand Gala Opening" of the Union, Luton, took place at 7.30 pm on Monday 11 October and on this occasion the ceremony was performed by the British film star Robert Douglas who was the star of the film "Our Fighting Navy" to be screened that evening and throughout the week. This was the first Opening at which the local mayor or another civic dignitary did not officiate. Another star present was the then well-known Chili Bouchier, and among others on stage was Leslie H. Kemp, Director of Theatre Construction. The stage show featured Terry's 26 Juveniles, a company of youngsters who between them presented a complete revue, with singing, dancing, comedy and speciality acts. Robinson Cleaver presided at the organ and also introduced the "In Town Tonight" feature which on this occasion included several popular personalities, among them representatives of Vauxhall Motors and the Luton Town Football Club.

It is interesting to note that, like the company's new cinema in nearby Dunstable, this cinema was called the Union rather than the Ritz. Its design and decoration followed the Company's well-established practice and the auditorium seated 2,104 patrons.

The Wurlitzer organ was the first of a new version to be ordered by Union Cinemas: whilst remaining a 3-manual 8-unit instrument, a heavier French Trumpet unit was supplied instead of the milder Style D trumpet unit employed hitherto and this was provided with a 16ft bass octave of pipes, thus producing an altogether "beefier" effect than had been available on previous models. Rather curiously, however, there was no "phantom" grand piano attachment. Speaking stops were spread over all three manuals, as at Chatham, and general pistons and other playing aids were also present. To the audience, the most striking visual change was the enlarged version of the "Pillar and Vase" illuminated surround for the console, the pillars themselves being doubled in width and embellished with a metal leaf motif running down the front of each one.

Robinson Cleaver remained at Luton for a second week and was followed by Arthur Manning and Rudy Lewis, with Harold Ramsay appearing for the week commencing 27 December.

The next edition of "Radio Rodeo" was broadcast from the Union, Kingston, at 9.00 pm on Wednesday 20 October and another strong bill included Harry Richman, Scott & Whaley, Jeanne de Casalis (whose comedy monologues featured the scatter-brained character Mrs. Feather), Issy Bonn (the Hebrew comedian and singer), Bennett & Williams, Gaby Valle, Fred Hudson and the Eight Step Sisters. Harold Ramsay, Robinson Cleaver and Phil Park were the organists, Sidney Torch not appearing on this occasion. Torch had given his last broadcast from Kingston on 12 October and then left the Company, making some guest appearances elsewhere prior to taking up an important new appointment with the Hyam Brothers, by whom he had been employed before joining Union Cinemas.

In addition to his broadcasts from the Union, Kingston, some of which had been afternoon transmissions given with paying audiences present, Sidney Torch had continued to make records for the Columbia label during his time with the Company: two 10" and two 12" records were issued, all made on on the Kingston organ. These were for the most part recordings of popular numbers of the day, including "Looking around corners for you", but one of the 12" discs was entitled "Napoleon - a Soldier's Vision" and told the story of the French Revolution and Napoleon's defeat at Waterloo as visualised by a soldier wounded in the battle. The story was narrated by Phil Park, with Torch providing appropriate musical accompaniment throughout, together with a final song by the baritone David Jenkins. This must have been one of the most comprehensive demonstrations of the Kingston Wurlitzer's resources ever recorded. The other 12" disc featured a medley of popular songs of 1937 but beginning and ending with his famous signature tune "I Want to Sing a Torch Song."

There were five "Radio Parade" broadcasts during October, transmitted by Radio Normandy, the featured organists now being Harold Ramsay, Phil Park and Jack Dowle. In addition, Harold Ramsay continued the "Around the Union Cinemas" three-times-a-week series of 15-minute broadcasts from Radio Normandy, together with the "Peter the Planter" series on Radio Luxembourg. He also broadcast twice for the BBC, while Robinson Cleaver gave two from Bexley Heath and, as mentioned above, Sidney Torch gave his last two broadcasts from Kingston (on 9th and 12th) before leaving the Company. Joseph Seal gave two from Belfast. Thus, with the "Radio Rodeo" show, there were on BBC and commercial radio a grand total of nineteen programmes and twenty-seven actual transmissions for October!

In mid-October the Associated British Picture Corporation announced that it had acquired a substantial holding of shares in Union Cinemas, amounting to 51% of the Ordinary and "A" Ordinary capital of the Company. It was further announced that two directors of ABPC would join the Board of Union Cinemas in substitution for existing directors and, as David Bernhard's place had not yet been filled, the effect of this would be that the new owners would take complete control. In the event, Frederick Bernhard and L.J.Clements both resigned on 31 October. They were replaced by W.D.Scrimgeour, a director of ABPC and Eric Lightfoot, secretary of the subsidiary company Associated British Cinemas Ltd. which would actually take over general management of the cinemas, with C.A.Davis as chairman

One of the first decisions to be taken by the new Board was that the quarterly dividend on the preference shares due on 31 December would not be paid (dividends on the first three quarters had been met and paid). Naturally, this news resulted in a serious drop in the Company's share prices: the First Preference fell 5s.1½d. to 10s.7½d., while the Second Preference fell 6s. to 8s.9d.; the Ordinary shares were also affected, as the prospect of dividends on these diminished.

It was obvious that the newly-constituted Board would be examining the day-to-day running of the Company's affairs very closely, as shareholders would be expecting a fully comprehensive statement at the first annual general meeting, due to take place towards the end of December.

One of the earliest signs of activity on the part of the new regime was the major cutback in press publicity. All over the country the characteristic white-on-black advertisement blocks carried in local newspapers ceased to appear after the second and third weeks on November, along with the wording "Union Cinemas" which had regularly appeared in them. At the cinemas themselves these references were quickly removed as well, though no attempt was made to change the names of the cinemas. For example, at Kingston the name "Union" remained in use for several months, only reverting to "Regal" in mid-June 1938.

In due course it became known that all work on new building was halted, with the exception of nine cinemas already under construction: Armagh would open in December, Hereford and Stockport in January, Hyde and Keighley in February, Hastings and Wigan in March, Kings Lynn in April and Richmond in May 1938. Rather curiously, however, announcements continued to be made in the trade press concerning future projects, so it would seem that the situation was regarded as purely temporary at this stage. Indeed, others were to follow, including Market Harborough in May 1939, Winchester in April 1940 and Bedminster in December 1940. All three of these were Union schemes for which the plans had been drawn up some time previously, so it would appear that in due course ABC decided that they fitted their own marketing programme.

The November "Radio Rodeo" broadcast was scheduled for Thursday 25 November, but was cancelled outright - presumably on the grounds of expense - nor was the show presented during the week on stage at the Union, Kingston. Instead, the stage show featured Rawicz and Landauer, a remarkable duo who used to play classical and lighter fare at two grand pianos placed facing each other; they possessed an astonishing rapport with each other and were regular broadcasters. However, Harold Ramsay had been appearing with the touring version of "Radio Rodeo" in recent weeks and the following week (commencing 29 November) the show was presented for the last time, at the Regal, Bexley Heath. By the same token, other stage shows continued to be presented at various cinemas on the circuit, though a steady reduction in the number of such shows soon became apparent.

Recordings of the "Radio Parade" shows from Radio Normandy continued for later transmission. In due course, the venue was switched from the Union, Kingston, to the Regal, Walham Green, an ABC cinema, although the programme schedules in Radio Pictorial continued to state that the show was presented "from the stage of the

Union Cinema, Kingston." After the series had been running for some weeks, the makers of Stork Margarine expressed an interest in sponsoring it and from 7 November onwards the show was given the new title "Stork Radio Parade." On the other hand, "Around the Union Cinemas" broadcasts continued to be presented by Union Cinemas Ltd. on Radio Normandy on Mondays, with repeats on Wednesdays and Saturdays, finally ending with the transmission on Wednesday 12 January 1938. Harold Ramsay continued the "Peter the Planter" broadcasts on Radio Luxembourg until 21 November, after which Robinson Cleaver took over from the Regal, Bexley Heath, the final broadcast in this series taking place on 27 February 1938.

During November Harold Ramsay gave three BBC broadcasts, one of them being to the Empire at 1.00 am on 4 November. Joseph Seal also gave three from Belfast and Robinson Cleaver two from Bexley Heath. It was evident that all three organists were established "regulars" so far as the BBC was concerned, and their radio appearances by now could no longer be seen as "plugs" for Union Cinemas, which they certainly had been in some quarters earlier on.

I have already described the involvement of William Southan Morris in the affairs of the Union Cinema Co., whereby the profitably-run circuit of which he was principal was amalgamated with the Union circuit in November 1933 for a consideration of £65,000. In August 1935 he was appointed General Manager of the Company. Later, I described his dismissal from this post one year later on his return from holiday in America, resulting in his decision to sue the Company for wrongful dismissal.

The case did not come to court until 22 November 1937, the hearing lasting for two days in the High Court, presided over by the Lord Chief Justice, Lord Hewart, with the great Sir Patrick Hastings KC appearing for the plaintiff.

It was revealed that prior to his departure on holiday Southan Morris had been on the most cordial of terms with the Directors, who had indeed wished him bon voyage. On his return, however, he found a letter awaiting him which contained ten allegations of breaches of duty. The ensuing meeting with the directors was described in Court as an "inquisitorial gathering", at the end of which he was dismissed. Among the charges levelled against him were that he failed to visit some of the cinemas, that he failed to attend adequately to bookings and that he had used the Company's time to attend to his own private affairs.

Southan Morris stated that while he was with the Company he had worked every day of the week and that although he had met with interference in all departments from Frederick Bernhard he had never received any complaints about his work until returning from his holiday in America.

Frederick Bernhard, under cross-examination, had to admit that after dismissing Southan Morris the Company had not replaced him with another General Manager; indeed, that one of the main objects of the dismissal had been to save £4,000 a year. As was to be expected, Southan Morris pointed out that the allegations made against him had been devised simply as a means to get rid of him from a post which was costing the Company £4,000 a year and which it had no intention of refilling.

In his summing-up the Lord Chief Justice drew attention to the two conflicting accounts presented by the defendant company: at one time Southan Morris was an example of energy and success and at another time he was "a miracle of slackness." They obviously had not thought of him as slack when they made the appointment, many months after they had first acquired his services, together with his profitable chain of cinemas.

For the defence, Sir William Jowitt KC argued that, having got the appointment, Southan Morris thought he could sit back and enjoy a "cushy" job instead of putting his back into things.

The jury found for the plaintiff and awarded him £11,000 with costs. Apparently Union Cinemas had already paid the sum of £5,000 into court, and the judge instructed that this be paid at once to Southan Morris or his solicitors. Incidentally, the foreman of the jury was Claude Hulbert, the well-known actor.

As a postscript, it is worth noting that Southan Morris went on after these events to pursue a successful career in the cinema business, setting up S.M.Enterprises Ltd. and developing another important circuit. One of the best-remembered of his achievements was the reopening of one of his most important cinemas, the Ritz, Birkenhead, on 13 January 1947, after it had suffered severe bomb damage during the war-time blitz. On that occasion, he demonstrated that he had lost none of his flair: the stage show included Billy Cotton and his Band and the organ was played by Robinson Cleaver and his wife Molly.

Another court case was to follow when E.R.Adams received one month's notice of dismissal from the position of Theatre Controller on 5 November. He decided to sue the Company for wrongful dismissal and in due course Mr Justice Stable ruled that in view of the importance of the position he held he was entitled to six months' notice and awarded him the rather curious sum of £1,381. This figure was calculated in part for the wrongful dismissal and in part for arrears of salary (which had been £2,000 per annum). Union Cinemas gave notice of appeal against this judgement.

Details of David Bernhard's estate were published in mid-November. He left £87,768 net, with an annuity of £3,000 to his widow if she continued to live at Windmill House, Shirley, dropping to £2,000 if she moved elsewhere and to £500 if she remarried. His important stamp collection was left to the Royal Philatelic Society.

C.A.Davis, who had been appointed chairman of Union Cinemas following the death of David Bernhard, resigned after the first few weeks and was replaced by John Maxwell himself, chairman of ABPC. He quickly announced that the new Board had appointed Peat, Marwick, Mitchell & Co. to make a complete investigation of the Company's affairs with a view to the preparation of a balance sheet as at 31 December, together with a Profit and Loss Account for the period from the original incorporation of the Company in December 1936 to 31 December 1937. Accounts prepared and signed by the Board in control directly after David Bernhard's death would be submitted to shareholders for information only but not for adoption, as the new Board found themselves unable to accept the value of the principal assets as shown therein. An independent valuation of these assets had also been ordered.

It was announced that the First Annual General Meeting of Union Cinemas Ltd. would be held on 22 December, at which time the fullest possible statement concerning the Company's affairs would be presented to shareholders. Some dramatic disclosures were made at this meeting by John Maxwell. He referred to the balance sheet as at 31 March 1937, in particular to the item "Freehold and leasehold properties, fixtures, fittings, furniture, plant, etc., at cost less realisation and reserve for amortisation of leasehold properties and depreciation: £3,865,564." Of this he remarked that it was the opinion of the new Board that the value was considerably higher than could be justified from their knowledge of the properties, from the point of view of either capital value or earning capacity. What the real value was, it was impossible to say at present, but in order to arrive at a proper figure arrangements had been made for an independent valuation to be undertaken.

Maxwell referred to the amalgamation of the three companies to form Union Cinemas Ltd. the previous December and said that the capital reconstruction involved had, in the opinion of the new Board, resulted in what he termed "share inflation" of some £2,200,000 which was entirely unjustified.

Another remarkable revelation was that in January 1936 a subsidiary company called Cinema Developments Ltd. had been formed, with a share capital of two shares of £1 each, owned by Union Cinemas Ltd. Cinema Developments were then loaned large sums of money to be used for the payment of salaries, allowances and expenses to directors and other officials and also to "negotiators" - presumably people concerned with locating sites for new cinema projects, obtaining planning approvals and so on. At the time of the balance sheet prepared for the period to 31 March 1937 the amount loaned in this way was some £60,000 and by 30 September a further amount of over £40,000 had been loaned! Just why these matters were dealt with in this way was not explained, but Maxwell advised the meeting that the bulk of the money involved would be chargeable to the profit and loss account.

Perhaps the most remarkable revelation of all, however, was that evidence had come to light of transactions involving transfers of assets to or from the Company, resulting in large profits or advantages accruing to various individuals at the ultimate expense of the Company. It was not possible for Maxwell to go into more detail, as fuller investigation needed to be made and it was possible that the transactions themselves might form the subject of legal proceedings at a later date. (This is a matter I did not set out to pursue in the course of my researches and in the event I did not stumble upon any further references to it).

As already announced, Peat, Marwick, Mitchell & Co. were making a complete investigation of the accounts, starting from the date of incorporation, and continuing the accounts right up to 31 December 1937 in order to cover a full year's working of the business. Their report would be presented at a special meeting, to be held in the Spring of 1938. Other steps taken included the cancellation of the building programme except for cinemas already under construction, the reduction of expenditure on advertising and exterior lighting of cinemas and the reduction of salaries and wages (which understandably had led to considerable unrest among the Company's employees). Naturally, in the circumstances, the payment of dividends on the preference shares (and hence the ordinary shares as well) was out of the question.

In the light of all this, one of the shareholders present, Sir Thomas Polson, proposed the setting up of a committee representing the interests of ordinary shareholders to assist the directors in their investigation of the company's affairs. He was supported by D.L.Sandelson, a solicitor, and after the meeting had closed these two gentlemen were appointed to a Committee of Investigation on behalf of preference and ordinary shareholders alike.

The chairman's resolution that the Report, as distinct from the accounts as at 31 March 1937, was put to the vote and carried unanimously, as was also a resolution proposing the adjournment of consideration of the accounts.

The touring edition of "Radio Rodeo" continued to visit selected cinemas during November. For the week commencing 1 November it was staged at the Ritz, Tunbridge Wells, with Harold Ramsay at the organ. The following week it was at the Ritz, Ipswich, but with Robinson Cleaver at the organ as Harold Ramsay was appearing at the Ritz, Belfast, for that cinema's First Birthday Week. Ramsay was back again for the week commencing 15 November when the show as at the Ritz, Cleethorpes. As mentioned already, the last date I have been able to establish was week commencing 29 November at the Regal, Bexley Heath, with Ramsay again.

About half a dozen other stage shows were also touring in November, reducing to about three in December. Another organist, Gordon Stanley, accompanied one such show.

So far as organists were concerned, touring was not normal ABC policy and so for the most part it ceased, resulting in residence being taken up at various cinemas around the circuit. Some stayed only until their contracts ran out. For example, Neville Meale found himself at the Ritz, Nuneaton, remaining there for some months and then leaving to take up free-lance work. There were some who continued with ABC: Arthur Manning was one of these, settling in at the Ritz, Barnsley, and in due course broadcasting from there. Peggy Weber, who had trained with Harold Ramsay and deputised for him on the touring editions of "Radio Rodeo", became resident at the Ritz, Penzance, in November. Gordon Banner was another who became resident in November: at the

Ritz, Oxford. Joseph Seal, of course, had already been resident at the Ritz, Belfast, for some time - indeed from the beginning of June - and was broadcasting regularly from there; he was to remain in Belfast for many years to come. Jack Dowle had been the last touring organist to appear at Belfast before this, and he himself then became resident at the Regal, Beckenham, at the beginning of June. However, at the end of November he transferred to the Ritz, Chatham, being replaced at Beckenham by Alex Taylor. Frank Matthew was at the Ritz, Ipswich, Barry Bretonner at the Ritz, Warrington, and Douglas Walker at the Luxor, Eastbourne.

Other organists took up short residencies prior to leaving to join other companies. Robinson Cleaver settled back at his old base theatre, the Regal, Bexley Heath, before leaving for the Granada at nearby Welling. Phil Park had been in charge of the Music Department at Kingston, but soon departed to go back to Hyams Brothers who appointed him to the Regal, Edmonton, where he commenced a long series of broadcasts. Dudley Savage was at the Adelphi, Slough, for several weeks before transferring to Plymouth for ABC.

There had been a training scheme for young organists during the year. One of these was Arthur Lord, who had trained with Robinson Cleaver: in December he became resident at the Rivoli, Southend. Another was Ray Baines, who had trained with Sidney Torch: he was posted to the Ritz, Barrow, in October. Raye Miller, a versatile young lady organist, was sent to the Regal, Uxbridge.

Apart from members of the Union team of organists, there was a gradual influx of new faces, some of them from Associated British Cinemas. Frank Slater became resident at the Ritz, Huddersfield, in November, later moving to the Ritz, Hereford, from where he eventually began to broadcast. Edwin Walton arrived at the Ritz, Aldershot, in December. Alfred Woods took over at the Ritz, Cleethorpes, and Basil Cuthbert at the Ritz, Horsham.

As already mentioned, Harold Ramsay himself continued to tour with the "Radio Rodeo" show until the end of November, after which he made appearances at various cinemas on the circuit and in due course at one or two of the ABC houses in the London area.

The first to be opened of the nine cinemas referred to as being under construction at the time of the take-over by ABPC was the Ritz, Armagh. Another small cinema, with 782 seats, this was opened on 6 December.

Although ABPC took control of the bulk of the Union Cinemas circuit, there were a few cinemas which were not included. Most importantly, the Tunbridge Wells group comprising the Ritz, Opera House, Kosmos and Great Hall remained outside the take-over and Frederick Bernhard continued to administer them.

What is certain is that after the take-over the new management looked closely at all of the leasing arrangements, contracts and so on connected with cinemas previously operated by Union Cinemas. Circumstances might come to light in which ABC decided to cancel such arrangements, leading eventually to the disposal of particular houses, and this would follow in due course.

CHAPTER TEN

THE STARS MOVE ON

Events in the year 1938 fall into three main divisions: the opening of the cinemas which were under construction at the time ABPC took control of Union Cinemas, together with a small number of future projects which were contemplated, activities and new appointments of various personalities - including organists - and the details contained in the report presented by John Maxwell at the meeting held on 5 May.

The second of the nine cinemas to be opened was the Ritz, Stockport, the ceremony taking place on 3 January. A 2,340-seater designed by Verity & Beverley, this cinema followed closely the lines of its predecessors, with spacious vestibule, beautifully decorated auditorium, well-equipped projection room, large stage with dressing rooms, café-restaurant and so on. The Wurlitzer organ, opened by ABC organist Wilfred Southworth, was the second of the new series of models introduced the previous October at the Union, Luton, featuring the French trumpet unit with 16ft bass, etc., but this time including a grand piano attachment. In due course it was to be broadcast by organist Frederick Haig.

Wilfred Southworth was at the organ again for the opening of the Ritz, Hereford, one week later, on 10 January. The ceremony was performed by the Mayor, with Leslie Kemp, the architect responsible for the design of the cinema, on stage with other company officials. The 1,012-seat auditorium was of the stadium type. An interesting feature was the ground floor café-restaurant which doubled for passengers using the bus station situated at the rear of the building. The Compton organ was the third and last to be built with the 2-

manual 4-unit plus Melotone specification, this time with the chamber located under the stage. Many visiting organists later declared it to be the best of the three. In due course, this organ also was to be broadcast by Frank Slater.

In January the one-time Theatre Controller and later Director of Theatre Construction at Union Cinemas, J.H.Lundy, was reported to have formed J.H.L. Theatres Ltd., his first acquisition being the Ritz, Potters Bar. The trade press also reported that he was conducting negotiations for 23 other cinemas.

Harold Ramsay was of course no longer Controller of Live Entertainment, but continued to tour for a time as the leading organist on the circuit: his first engagement in January was at the Ritz, Horsham. Presently, however, he made appearances at one or two ABC cinemas as distinct from those under Union Cinemas control. For example, the week commencing 24 January saw him at the Mayfair, Upper Tooting, playing the 3-manual 9-unit Christie organ there. This was not very far away from the famous Granada, Tooting, where he had enjoyed his first success in this country, and it may be that this was an attempt to cash in on his popularity in the district. His last broadcasts from the Union, Kingston, were given on 4, 11, 18 and 27 January. Meanwhile, he was preparing to leave the Company in order to launch his next venture: a tour of variety theatres with a Hammond/Lafleur pipeless electric organ. He later wrote that the "Radio Rodeo" shows and other stage presentations had introduced him to a completely new audience and that he would be able to capitalise on this. Thanks to sponsorship, commercial radio continued to flourish: the "Stork Radio Parade" weekly variety shows with organ accompaniment were broadcast from Radio Normandy (with repeats on Wednesday mornings on Radio Luxembourg for several weeks) until mid-April. Presumably the arrangements with ABC were terminated at that point, as thereafter the programme was renamed "Stork Radio Parade - Second Edition" and recorded for broadcasting at various Granada Theatres, Bobby Howell and his Band replacing the organ. On 9 January Harold Ramsay himself began another series on Radio Normandy, billed as "Harold Ramsay at the Organ" and sponsored by the makers of Fynnon Salt, destined for a long run.

Much the same could be said of Robinson Cleaver: having joined Granada, his first task was to preside at the Wurlitzer organ at the opening on 2 February of the Granada, Welling, situated quite close to Bexley Heath, where he had enjoyed such great popularity at the Regal.

Apparently, he was accorded the warmest of welcomes there, being carried into the cinema shoulder-high by a large gathering of enthusiastic fans. Incidentally, his first Granada broadcast was from Clapham Junction on 24 February, after which regular broadcasts from Welling started a few weeks later, on 23 April. He was to remain with Granada for almost twenty years.

As previously mentioned, Sidney Torch had already left the Company. In due course he was to preside at the large Wurlitzer organ at the Opening of the Gaumont State, Kilburn, on 20 December 1937. His first solo broadcast from Kilburn was on 10 January. Before this, however, he had found time for some other engagements, notably the Opening of the Compton organ installed in the Theatre Royal, Halifax, on 7 December.

The trade press also reported in January that Phil Park, having resigned from Union Cinemas where he had been in charge of the Music Department, had been appointed organist at the large Hyams Brothers cinema, the Regal, Edmonton, in succession to Frank Newman and commencing on 17 January. In due course he began regular broadcasts from that theatre. Previously, he had broadcast mainly at the BBC Theatre Organ, with one isolated transmission from the Regal, Bexley Heath; other than that, he had of course gone on the air as one of the pianists on the "Radio Rodeo" shows, for which he had also written the continuity and special lyrics.

On 24 January Jack Dowle became resident organist at the Union, Kingston. The name of this cinema eventually reverted to the Regal on 13 June.

At the beginning of February Union Cinemas lost another court action, this one being brought against them by a company called Industrial and Equitable Advertising Films Ltd. The plaintiffs claimed that Union Cinemas had broken three contracts for the showing of films and slide advertisements, one dated 16 July 1937 for local advertisements, one dated 4 August 1937 for national advertisements, and one concerning their right to exercise an option under an agreement dated 31 July 1937 to continue for a further 52 weeks. Union Cinemas counter-claimed that only the first contract was valid, but lost the case.

During February there was considerable debate concerning the future of stage shows presented in cinemas. It seemed that much turned upon whether the cinema industry should accumulate large profits by offering its customers nothing more tangible than a series of projected images and whether the presentation of variety acts on stage would provide a contrast against which the films themselves might compare unfavourably.

Several of the large cinema circuits regularly promoted stage shows in their major cinemas and when Union Cinemas came under the control of John Maxwell this was obviously an aspect of their programming which came under scrutiny. There were contracts still running and these were looked at closely, but on the whole it appeared doubtful whether they would be renewed. It was nevertheless appreciated that circumstances could vary in different parts of the country and according to the type of people from whom the cinema's patronage was drawn.

One very important decision was certainly taken at about this time: that there would be an end to broadcasts of variety shows from cinema stages. On 14 December a lavish stage show had been broadcast by the BBC from the Dominion, Tottenham Court Road, London, with Jessie Matthews top of the bill, together with the Western Brothers, Murray & Mooney, Louis Levy and his Gaumont British Symphony Orchestra and Fredric Bayco at the organ. This was followed by the broadcasting of the Opening of the Gaumont State, Kilburn, in which Gracie Fields, George Formby, Larry Adler, Vic Oliver and others took part, together with Alfred Van Dam and his Orchestra and Sidney Torch at the organ. Apparently there was alleged to have been a significant drop in attendances at cinemas in many parts of the country on the evenings when these two broadcasts took place. Both were of course Gaumont British enterprises and it is perhaps of interest to note that there had been little or no evidence to suggest that the monthly "Radio Rodeo" broadcasts from the Union, Kingston, in 1937 had produced a similar effect.

Cinema organ broadcasts during this period were immensely popular, drawing very large radio audiences, and a goodly number of the organists involved enjoyed "star" status and were as much "household names" as most of the popular dance band leaders of the day. The Granada circuit ran an annual questionnaire to be completed by its audiences and this revealed that up to 80% were in favour of organ music as part of the cinema programme.

On 21 February the Ritz, Hyde, was opened. Designed by W.T.Benslyn, this was another of the smaller houses, with seating for 1,256 patrons. A striking feature of the entrance was the large cream and red canopy, 36ft long and 19ft deep. The vestibule was decorated in a buff stone colour and the auditorium walls were spray-painted in Chinese orange and gold. The drapes were in maroon and the seats were red. Projection equipment included Ross projectors and RCA High-Fidelity sound system.

The Ritz, Keighley, was opened by the Mayor on 28 February in the presence of A.S.Moss, General Manager of ABC. It was another Verity & Beverley cinema designed on typical Union lines and S. Beverley was also present. The outside elevations of the building were in rustic red brick. The auditorium, with stalls and balcony seating for 1,526 patrons, was decorated in old rose and gold. As one would expect, the stage was of large size in anticipation of Cine-Variety performances. Of particular interest was the fact that the Compton organ, opened by Wilfred Southworth, was the 3-manual 5-unit instrument originally installed at the Regal, Oxford, in April 1937 - less than a year earlier! At Keighley the organ chambers were under the stage, all of the pipework being in the right hand chamber and the Melotone being in the left hand one. The console, complete with its "Pillar and Vase" illuminated surround, was mounted on a lift in the centre of the orchestra pit. A café-restaurant seating 100 was also provided.

The next major cinema to be opened was the Ritz, Wigan, on 7 March, the Mayor officiating with A.S.Moss again in attendance, together with a number of local dignitaries. The architects were John Fairweather & Son, of Glasgow, the original scheme having been planned by Green's Playhouse Ltd., a company noted for very large cinema projects in Scotland. With 2,560 seats, the Wigan auditorium would have been the largest to be owned by Union Cinemas had it been ready before ABPC took control. Interestingly, the organ originally intended for the Ritz, a Wurlitzer of similar specification to that at the Ritz, Stockport, was not installed there - although the chambers had been built for it - but diverted for use elsewhere.

The Ritz, Hastings, opened on 19 March, was another cinema to be designed by Verity & Beverley for Union Cinemas and followed the well-established style of architecture and decoration adopted by the Company. Seating was provided for 1,906 patrons in the spacious auditorium. Interestingly, the house tabs supplied for the stage were of ABC type. Once again, the Wurlitzer organ was opened by Wilfred Southworth.

As a matter of interest, this particular organ had been despatched from the Wurlitzer factory almost a year earlier (27 March 1937) and was

Harold Ramsay, Union Kingston.
Photo: Author's Collection.

Dudley Savage, Kingsway Levenshulme.
Photo: Tony Moss Collection.

Joseph Seal, Ritz Belfast.
Photo: John D. Sharp Collection.

Hubert Selby, Ritz Richmond.
Photo: Author's Collection.

Rudy Lewis, Capitol Didsbury.
Photo: John D. Sharp Collection.

Frank Matthew, Ritz Belfast.
Photo: Author's Collection.

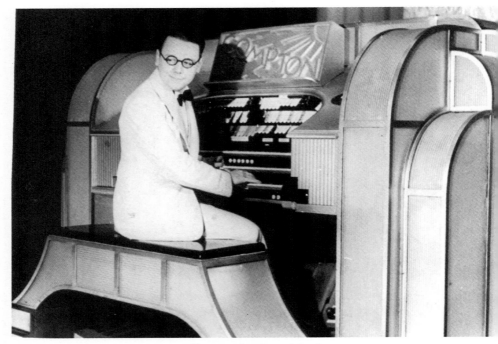

Neville Meale, Ritz Maidstone.
Photo: John D. Sharp Collection.

Phil Park, Union Kingston.
Photo: Author's Collection.

3/8 Wurlitzer with Mk. II surround, Ritz Luton.
Photo: John D. Sharp Collection

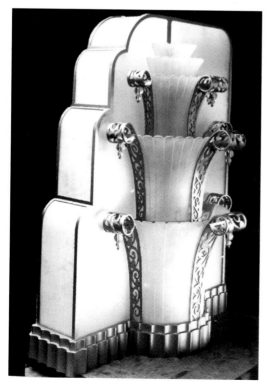

"Pillar & Vase" MK 11 illuminated
console end by R.R. Beard Ltd.
Photo: Author's Collection.

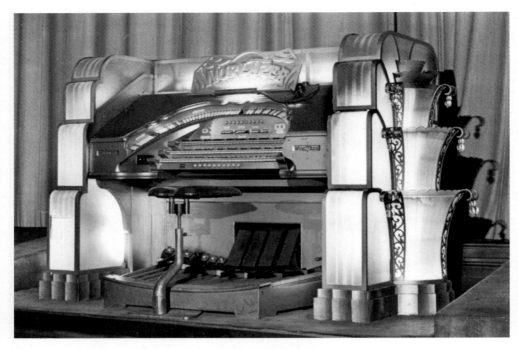

3/7 Wurlitzer , Ritz Aldershot.
Photo: John D. Sharp Collection.

2/4 Compton, Ritz Penzance.
Photo: John D. Sharp Collection.

Alex Taylor, Union Luton.
Photo: Tony Moss Collection.

Sidney Torch,
Ritz Barnsley.
Photo: Author's
Collection.

3/8 Wurlitzer with grand piano on separate lift, Ritz Chatham.
Photo: John D. Sharp Collection.

The second meeting of the Cinema Organ Society. Douglas Badham and Hubert
Selby at the organ with the Author in the background, Ritz Chatham.
Photo: Author's Collection.

built to the original specification drawn up by Harold Ramsay and first introduced at the Ritz, Ipswich, but with the "phantom" grand piano omitted. In the absence of any evidence to the contrary, a possible explanation for this may be that following the success of the first Wurlitzer ordered by Union Cinemas for the Ritz, Huddersfield, the next order to be placed was for four more organs based on this model with the modifications called for by Harold Ramsay after his appointment as Musical Director. The first three were destined for Ipswich, Barnsley and Aldershot, with the fourth perhaps intended for Chatham. However, as the Ritz, Chatham, was planned to be "Kent's largest cinema", it is possible that the decision was taken to upgrade the organ to a fully-unified 3-manual instrument which could have been specially ordered separately a short time later. This would have left the fourth organ on order for use elsewhere at some future date. That it was despatched from the Wurlitzer factory when it was would seem to add some weight to this theory, though the despatch list did indicate that it was intended for Hastings. Presumably it had been realised that the first order needed to be completed and that the London factory should agree to keep the organ in store. It should be noted that this is pure speculation on my part, but it is worth pointing out that the instruments on the next order - for Luton, Stockport and Wigan - represented an improved version of the Chatham 3-manual Special rather than more of the first type and indeed the one for Luton was despatched on the same day as the one for Hastings: 27 March 1937. Rather than the opus numbers, despatch dates and so on, what seems the more significant is the actual sequence of orders and when they were placed.

The Theatre Royal, King's Lynn, had been severely damaged by fire in 1936, and was rebuilt and reopened without ceremony on 4 April. The architect responsible for the new building was Keeble Allflatt and initially it was operated on a lease, only being purchased outright in 1946.

The new Board of Union Cinemas having been reported as halting the building programme except for a number of cinemas already under construction, it was somewhat curious to find that new projects continued to be reported in the trade press. References were made in March to a new Ritz to be built at Burnley, with Leslie H. Kemp as architect, and to another at Welling, with the firm of Harringtons as architects.

The complete investigation carried out by the chartered accountants Peat, Marwick, Mitchell & Co. ordered by John Maxwell when he assumed control of Union Cinemas Ltd. was concluded in the Spring, together with a valuation as at 31 December 1937 made by cinema valuers Messrs. Harris & Gillow. The first details to be released were published at the beginning of May and revealed that a total of £3,192,629 had been placed in a suspense account, this being the amount not represented by any available assets. This figure broke down as follows:

"Writing up" of book values of cinema properties on acquisition from the liquidated companies:	£2,181,020
Further deficiency on revaluation of cinema properties:	£ 527,817
Deficiency on revaluation on investments in and amounts due by subsidiary and associated companies:	£ 393,215
Deficiency on the liquidation of two subsidiary companies:	£ 22,849
Cinema development expenditure, provision for legal action against the company, the investigation and valuation expenses, losses on abortive schemes and other sundry losses:	£ 90,341
Less capital reserve:	£ 22,613
	£3,192,629

The total of the balance sheet was £5,768,260; the issued capital was £3,265,026; thus to all intents and purposes the share capital of the company had been lost.

At the adjourned Meeting held on 5 May, John Maxwell went through the Suspense Account item by item. Regarding the assets of the company having been written up too high, he said that this sum appeared to have been reached without any attempt to apportion the total value over the individual properties of the company. He could not understand how the overvaluation could have arisen, but assumed that it was due to what he considered to be the absurdly high market prices of the three companies being merged, as quoted on the Stock Exchange at the time of the merger. The £1 shares of the old Union Cinema Company were being quoted at around £12 and forty-nine 5s. shares were given in exchange for each £1 share. At the same time, three 5s. shares were given for each 5s. share of Oxford & Berkshire Cinemas Ltd. and four 5s. shares were given for each 5s. share of National Provincial Cinemas Ltd. These arrangements did indeed seem to be based on the stock market prices at the time, but how those prices had ever risen so high was something Maxwell could not fathom and he went on to say that he could see absolutely no justification for them having done so.

Maxwell went on to state that when Oxford & Berkshire Cinemas Ltd. was formed, a number of properties were transferred to it from the Union Cinema Co. at prices greatly in excess of their actual cost. This was therefore a straightforward inflation of their value. He also said that as a result of various transactions between directors and officials of the company, other properties were taken over by the company for sums in excess of their actual cost, resulting in their book costs being inflated beyond real values; consequently it had been necessary in the revaluation to mark these costs down to a value corresponding to their profit-earning capacity. The "intermediate" profits that had been made were unjustified.

A further problem had been identified, resulting from policy decisions in regard to purchases and new construction. Without naming the town concerned (obviously Horsham) he gave as his example the purchase of three existing cinemas in order to achieve a monopoly in the town and thereby to obtain films on a cheaper hire basis, only to discover that another company (Odeon Theatres) was planning to build a new cinema in the same town, and then taking the decision to build a new one themselves (and getting it open first). The final result was of course that a town with a population of around 14,000 ended up with five cinemas and serious over-seating, so that in due course two of the original three cinemas had to be closed down. With the subsequent revaluation, the value of the remaining old cinema had to be written down very considerably and in addition the cost of the new one had been greatly in excess of its value in terms of earning capacity. The total shrinkage resulting in this one instance was more than £40,000 and according to Maxwell there were other cases of this kind in various parts of the country. The cost of building new cinemas in small and medium-sized towns could in several instances not be justified in terms of their actual profitability. To that extent the policy of expansion pursued by Union Cinemas could only be seen as defective.

The situation arrived at clearly indicated that the issued capital of £3,265,026 would have to bear the brunt of the deficiency shown in the Suspense Account. Having taken control of Union Cinemas, with all its problems, John Maxwell could only advise shareholders that the business would have to be carefully nursed along and he proposed that any attempt to reconstruct the company's capital position should be left for twelve months in order to ascertain the real earning power of the assets under what he considered to be normal trading conditions. Meanwhile, he referred to some of the activities of members of the old management as being highly improper and indeed injurious to the interests of shareholders, but because of possible legal action did not go into details.

Answering questions from shareholders, Maxwell countered suggestions that the revaluation had been too drastic by declaring that it was a genuine and honest valuation carried out by professionals specialising in the field. Frederick Bernhard complained that he knew the investigation had been completed some time previous to the meeting, but that nevertheless Maxwell had not thought fit to supply him with any of its details, either to himself directly or to any other past officers of the company whose conduct had been called into question. Maxwell replied that the details had been supplied to Mr. Davis, Mr. Bernhard's lawyer, to which Bernhard then stated that Mr Davis was not his lawyer. Maxwell replied that he could go into those details in the courts. From this one may presume that Mr. Davis, who had been chairman for a short time after David Bernhard's death but then resigned, had either not been very effective in that role, in which case he might well have been asked to resign by Maxwell, or had seen enough to realise that the company's affairs had not been conducted as well as they should have been, and so resigned anyway. I myself tend to the latter view, as he had evidently felt disinclined to pass on to Frederick Bernhard any of the information Maxwell said he had given him after the investigation.

In retrospect, one may also ask just how much Maxwell himself knew about the company when he acquired the shares which gave him control. The share prices had dropped substantially in the wake of David Bernhard's death and he may have thought he was getting a bargain at that time, adding a number of modern cinemas to his existing ABC circuit and no doubt getting rid of many of the old ones. It may be that only later did he discover that there were serious managerial and financial problems that had to be faced. On the other hand, as one of the most important cinema magnates of the day he must have been reasonably aware of the history of the Union Cinemas project right from its very beginning and one feels that he must surely have had some inkling of what he was taking on. As it was, having acquired control, he now had to placate the shareholders as best he could, and it is probably true to say that his strong approach to the situation and the decisions he took to deal with it were the fairest and the most reasonable in the circumstances.

It appears that it was originally planned that the Ritz, Richmond, should replace the Union, Kingston, as the flagship of the circuit and to this end it was to be provided with the most elaborate equipment. This was to include a large stage complete with fly-tower and a suite of twelve dressing rooms, together with a special Wurlitzer organ which with 16 units was to be twice the size of the various standard types installed hitherto - almost certainly Harold Ramsay would have drawn up a specification very similar to that planned for the Granada, Manchester, ownership of which passed to Gaumont-British shortly before the opening. The Music Department under Phil Park's management would also be transferred there from Kingston. However, none of this was to be. Once the company had passed into ABPC control, these extra-lavish arrangements were cancelled outright. The stage end of the building was finished by the simple expedient of dropping a back wall behind the screen. The large Wurlitzer organ was cancelled and in due course was replaced by the 8-unit instrument which had been ordered for the Ritz, Wigan: this arrived at Richmond without its grand piano attachment - although the stopkeys and expression controls for it were present on the console. A considerable period was to elapse first, but eventually the instrument was to be broadcast a great deal, and by many different organists.

The Ritz, Richmond, eventually opened on 19 May. Once again, Wilfred Southworth was at the organ. The architects were Verity & Beverley, working in association with Leslie H. Kemp. Situated in Sheen Road, the facade of the building was rendered in neo-Georgian style in brick and stone, harmonising well with the traditional architecture of the town. There was the usual double row of entrance doors to provide a draught lobby before reaching the main vestibule with its grand staircase. The auditorium, seating 2,150, was decorated in peach, gold and pastel blue. The proscenium curtains were a special feature, having been designed by Leslie Kemp, and were in white silk velvet embroidered with gold and blue satin, and trimmed with gold fringe. The projection room equipment included two Ross projectors and high intensity arcs, together with RCA sound apparatus. There was also a large and smartly-furnished café-restaurant, the front end of the building having been virtually completed by the time of the take-over.

It is understood that the original scheme also provided for demolition of certain buildings opposite the cinema so as to afford an unobstructed view of the facade from the town centre, but obviously this, too, was cancelled. Instead, an illuminated sign with a moving arrow indicating that the Ritz was "around the corner" was installed in a convenient location.

In June announcements were made concerning three more new cinemas to be added to the circuit. One of these was the "long awaited" small cinema to be erected at Market Harborough. The architect was W.T.Benslyn, in collaboration with Leslie Kemp, and the cinema was to seat 1,020 patrons. This cinema, called the Ritz as usual, did not open its doors until May 1939.

The other two projects were stated to be at King James's Road in King's Lynn, where a site was being cleared and tenders from building contractors would be invited in due course; and at Uxbridge, where it was reported that building had already commenced. I can find no further record of these projects. It is curious that the trade press continued to publish information of this kind despite the known policy of the ABC Management.

CHAPTER ELEVEN

BALANCING ACT

Occasionally decisions were taken to dispose of certain cinemas operating under Union Cinemas control. One of these was the Ritz, Tonbridge, which passed to an independent exhibitor on 21 February 1939. Additionally, cinemas which had been leased from South Wales Cinemas in March 1937, including the Knowle Hall and Windsor, Neath, and the Albert Hall, Carlton and Picture House, Swansea, were returned to that company with effect from 1 October 1939.

The Ritz, Winchester, opened without ceremony on 29 April 1940. It is interesting to note that it had been included in a list of cinemas "nearing completion" published as early as August 1937 - evidence, perhaps, of the extraordinary optimism displayed so frequently by Union Cinemas in its publicity campaigns. Clearly it was a project which had already been planned but which for various reasons had been long delayed before being brought to fruition. Evidently ABC were prepared to arrange for the work to go ahead and to open the cinema in due course as one of their own houses

Situated in Middle Brook Street, off the High Street, the Ritz was finished with a mellow brick frontage with dwarf towers at each end. The four pairs of double doors gave onto a foyer with the relatively low ceiling typical of Union practice, leading to the 1,500-seat auditorium comprising stalls and balcony. The stage was deep but without dressing room facilities. It seems likely that the original plans did in fact include such provision and that an organ was specified but ABC cancelled these items. Indeed, war-time conditions may well have influenced the company in reaching this decision

119

The "long awaited" cinema in Market Harborough was finally opened on 22 May by Sir Arthur Hazelrigg, Lord Lieutenant of Leicestershire. Built to the plans of W.T.Benslyn FRIBA, with E.F.Tulley acting as consultant, this was another of the smaller cinemas, with 1,020 seats (later revised to 1,109). Although the plans had been drawn up before the arrival of ABPC on the scene, building work was not actually started in this instance and consequently the project was postponed by the new management. The award of the building contract was eventually announced in the trade press in June 1938.

Although officially still owned by Union Cinemas, the familiar ABC logo sign consisting of an inverted triangle enclosing the letters "ABC" was in evidence on the outside of the building, but with the words "Managed by" added above. Local press advertisement blocks were treated in the same manner. The first manager for the new cinema was F.V.Walford, transferring from the Regal, Derby. In the trade press the opening was described as "ABC's third in 3 weeks." So far as the general public was concerned, this was indeed an ABC house; the continued existence of Union Cinemas as the owning company was not publicised.

As reported earlier, E.R.Adams, who had been appointed Theatre Controller in June 1937, was among those given notice almost immediately after ABC had taken over. As this was an important management role, Mr Adams felt that the one month's notice he had been given in a somewhat peremptory manner was inappropriate and that he should sue for wrongful dismissal. In court, Mr Justice Stable had decided that six months' notice should have been given and had awarded him the sum of £1,381 covering arrears of salary plus compensation for the wrongful dismissal.

Union Cinemas, under its new Board of Directors, gave notice of appeal against this decision and the matter was brought before the Court of Appeal on 25 May 1939. Lord Justice MacKinnon presided, together with Lord Justice du Parcq and Mr Justice Atkinson. The basis of the appeal was that the contract had been oral but that there had been no written memorandum of the contract to satisfy the Statute of Frauds and the contract was therefore unenforceable. Lord Justice MacKinnon said that he did not think there had been any definite agreement for two years, nor had there been a yearly hiring; therefore the Statute of Frauds could not apply in this case. He thought there was clearly an agreement for Mr Adams to perform the duties of Theatre Controller for an indefinite period until a written agreement had been prepared, which could have taken some time. Having regard to the nature and importance of the appointment, he considered that Mr Adams was entitled to a reasonable notice and agreed that the six months ruled by the trial judge was both reasonable and proper. The appeal was dismissed without calling on counsel for the respondent and leave to appeal to the House of Lords was refused.

The second Annual General Meeting of shareholders took place on 30 June 1939. John Maxwell stated that the trading profit for 1938 had been £203.500 representing an increase of £58,000 on 1937. After deduction of £110,400 in respect of interest, £23,500 for tax and £50,000 for depreciation, this left £19,600 to be carried forward, compared with £8,700 the previous year. The suspense account remained at £3,192,629 as before, to be regarded as having no value. Liabilities were in the region of £2,165,000 and assets around £300,000. The preference shares remained in dividend arrears.

John Maxwell reported a gradual improvement in the overall situation, but said that with such massive floating debts it would take a long time to achieve the earning power necessary to bring about any serious reduction of the liabilities. There would be no point in attempting a reconstruction scheme to alter the share capital structure to meet capital losses but which did not provide for funding or stabilisation of the floating debts.

Meanwhile, the new Board had been concentrating on disentangling the complicated structure of associated and subsidiary companies in order to bring everything together in the parent company: ten of them had been liquidated during the year, with another thirty or so remaining!

A large number of claims and legal actions against the company, arising out of various contracts or alleged contracts, had already been dealt with. The reserve in respect of actions still pending had been reduced by some £5.000 and now stood at £20,000, with a considerable number of outstanding claims still outstanding. Substantial provision had been made for liability arising from the liquidation of subsidiary companies.

The increased profit for the year was considered satisfactory, with much of the improvement coming from cinemas opened in 1937 and 1938, although the latter openings naturally did not reflect a full year's trading results. The first half of the year was to be regarded as a "cleaning up" period, with most of the improvements coming in the second half.

Messrs. Maxwell, Scrimgeour and Lightfoot were re-elected to the Board and the shareholders who were present evidently expressed confidence that things would continue to improve, albeit slowly. On the other hand, share prices having dropped appreciably after the take-over had levelled out and remained fairly steady: in the first week of July, the Ordinary stood at 7½d., the First Preference at 3s.1½d. and the Second Preference at 1s.3d.

The subsidiary company called Union Cinemas Subsidiary Properties Ltd. had been floated in June 1937, acquiring a number of cinemas in various parts of the country, mostly from another subsidiary, Alliance Cinemas Ltd. These cinemas were to be leased to Union Cinemas Ltd., rentals due thereby providing the new company's income. A large mortgage had been taken out, together with a sinking fund arrangement to redeem the mortgage - if still outstanding - by the end of September 1985.

The management of Union Cinemas Ltd. having been taken over by ABC at the end of October 1937, a new temporary arrangement was made between Union Cinemas and ABC whereby Subsidiary Properties would receive as rent the net earnings of the cinemas leased to the parent company, with a specified minimum sum each half-year. The arrangement was to be considered a temporary one with an expiry date of 31 December 1939. Under the arrangement, the amount received from Union Cinemas for the year to 30 June was £59,068 (as against £71,003 the previous year). Having paid mortgage interest and administrative expenses, the profit was £27,645 (as against £37,803). To this was added £8,117 transferred from contingency reserve. Then, after tax, transfer to reserve fund for mortgage redemption, payment of dividends, etc., there remained a balance of £7,190 to be carried forward.

However, it was revealed that the directors had not yet been able to negotiate a permanent settlement of the relationship with Union Cinemas Ltd. In July 1939 L.J.Clements had resigned and two other directors, one of them Sir Frederick Field, retiring by rotation did not offer themselves for re-election. At the request of Union Cinemas, Messrs. Scrimgeour and Lightfoot were proposed. During the year the auditors also resigned.

Dividends on the 6% cumulative participating preference shares in Union Cinemas Subsidiary Properties Ltd. were paid on 30 April 1940. Thus, despite the continuing uncertainty regarding the relationship with Union Cinemas Ltd. and the various resignations, etc., which had

122

taken place in the summer of 1939, this company was seen to be trading at a reasonably satisfactory level.

In July it was announced that the respective managements found it desirable to settle matters between them. The rental payable by Union Cinemas, currently running at £89,262 per annum, was to be reduced to £63,000. This latter figure was calculated to be sufficient to cover all interest and redemption charges. A loan of £45,000 from Subsidiary Properties to Union Cinemas was to be cancelled and the rate of mortgage redemption was to be increased. A further proposal was that a new company should be formed to take over the existing company's cinemas and equipment, together with the sinking fund policy (with the Equity and Law Life Assurance Society). Holders of the 6% cumulative preference shares in Subsidiary Properties would be offered 6% debenture stock in the new company on a pound for pound basis. Redemption of the stock would be made by means of a 1% cumulative sinking fund. Meetings would be held in August to consider these proposals.

There was some delay in publication of the trading results of Union Cinemas Ltd. for 1939, due in June 1940, owing to the indisposition of the chairman, John Maxwell. However, details were announced in August and showed that the trading profit had held up remarkably well, amounting to £195,399 as against £203,524 for 1938. Having regard to the outbreak of war and its consequent effect on the cinema industry during the latter part of the year, this figure was considered by no means unsatisfactory.

After payment of interest and provision for income tax, depreciation and amortisation, the net profit was £12,109 which, with £28,317 brought forward, produced a total of £40,425 to be carried forward to the next account. The reserve held in respect of legal actions pending against the company was reduced from £20,000 to £8,000. The assets, fixtures, etc., continued to be based on the valuation made as at 31 December 1937. The suspense account had been reduced by £78,274 but the auditors repeated that no value attached to this item.

Though perhaps not strictly relevant to our story, it is worth noting that the decision was announced in September that no dividend would be paid to ordinary shareholders in ABPC for the year to March 1940, the reason given being that it was considered necessary to conserve resources in view of increased enemy activity leading to lower cinema receipts.

John Maxwell, the chairman, died on 2 October 1940 aged 63 years. He was without doubt one of the most outstanding figures in the history of the British film and cinema industry. His career and remarkable achievements have been well documented elsewhere, but what is perhaps not widely known today is that in 1936 he had taken steps with a view to possibly obtaining control of the Gaumont-British Picture Corporation. Against formidable American competition he acquired a large holding of "B" shares which entitled him to a five-year option on acquiring 51% of the "A" shares in Metropolis & Bradford Trust Ltd. which held the controlling shares in Gaumont-British. At the very least this gives some indication of the strength and determination with which Maxwell approached business affairs. As we have seen, in the following year he acquired control of Union Cinemas, a major coup by any standards, notwithstanding the substantial problems which followed in its wake.

A new company, Union Cinemas Investments Ltd., was registered on 3 October 1940 with a nominal capital of £1,000 in 1,000 shares of £1 each. Its object was to take over the seventeen cinemas, together with all fixtures and fittings and equipment pertaining to them, previously owned by Union Cinemas Subsidiary Properties Ltd., in accordance with the terms agreed between that company, Union Cinemas Ltd., Associated British Pictures Ltd. and the Equity and Law Life Assurance Society Ltd. to which I have already referred.

On the whole, Union Cinemas did not suffer too badly from enemy bombing during the War, but one serious incident occurred on the night of 15/16 October 1940 when the Regal, Kingston, received a direct hit at the stage end by a relatively small high explosive bomb, causing a considerable amount of damage. However, the structure of the building stood up to it well and after tremendous efforts had been made to clear up, the cinema was able to re-open on 16 December.

Another long-delayed project, the Ritz, Bedminster, Bristol, was opened on Monday 16 December 1940. Although the plans had been drawn up by Verity & Beverley well before ABPC had taken control, it would appear that this was one of the schemes in the Union Cinemas building programme which, because construction work on it had not really begun, was cancelled. However, second thoughts evidently prevailed and the decision was taken to build the cinema in a modified form arranged by ABC architect William Glen and to open it under ABC management.

The original plans had provided for a balcony, but due to wartime conditions this was not proceeded with - though the balcony was indeed added several years after the war had ended. Thus the auditorium as built consisted of stalls only with 1,250 seats. Typical ABC decor was applied. The equipment included two Ross projectors and Western Electric Mirrophone sound.

An extraordinary general meeting of Union Cinemas Subsidiary Properties Ltd. was held on 13 February 1941 to consider the resolution that the company be wound up voluntarily. This followed naturally from the setting up of the new company, Union Cinemas Investments Ltd., for the purpose of taking over the seventeen cinemas previously owned. The liquidator was named as J.H.McDonald of Hanover Square, London.

In July 1941 the new chairman of Union Cinemas Ltd., Mr R.G.Simpson, was able to report that the trading profit of the company in 1940 was £284,114 - a substantial increase over the previous year. After deduction of interest, the sum set aside for taxation was £95,000 and for depreciation and amortisation the sum was £60,000. With the balance brought forward from the previous year, this left £65,008 and after provision of £25,000 for War Damage premiums there remained £40,008 to be carried forward.

The increase in gross profit was largely attributable to increased earnings in certain parts of the country where war-time conditions (large concentrations of service personnel, etc.) had actually helped in those areas. In addition, there had been a decrease in the loss incurred by one of the subsidiary companies. There had also been a restriction on expenditure on running repairs and decorations, although the budget for this had been increased in the previous year.

The chairman was also able to announce that the bank overdraft had been reduced from £1,413,812 to £1,270,883.

Having dealt with the situation regarding Union Cinemas Subsidiary Properties, the amount due to subsidiary companies had been greatly reduced as well.

All in all, with a certain amount of luck and with careful administration by the new management, it could be said that good progress was being made in restoring the company's fortunes.

In October 1941 it was announced that ABPC would once again withhold dividends. At the Annual General Meeting soon afterwards there was strong criticism of this decision from the shareholders, on the basis that the finances of the company were strong and healthy, the money was there and the amount required for payment could easily be afforded. However, the chairman on this occasion, Sir Ralph Wedgwood, formerly chief of the London & North Eastern Railway, rejected these criticisms and pointed out that cinema attendances were low and it was necessary for the company to conserve its resources having regard to the uncertainties of war-time conditions.

In this connection, it is interesting to note that share prices in Union Cinemas during this period were actually rising. In October, the Ordinary stood at 8d., the First Preference at 6s.6d. and the Second Preference at 3s.6d. per share. This improvement was to continue in the months ahead, the preference shares in particular attracting a good deal of attention in the market. The following table shows the trend over the period from April to August 1942:

	April	May	June	July	August
Ordinary	1s.0d.	1s.4½d.	1s.7½d.	2s.1d.	2s.6d.
1st Preference	8s.10½.	12s.0d.	15s.6d.	17s.7½d.	18s.6d.
2nd Preference	5s.0d.	9s.0d.	11s.6d.	15s.7½d.	17s.9d.

Bearing in mind that no dividends had been paid since 1937, this performance would seem to indicate a considerable degree of confidence, especially on the part of preference shareholders, that under ABPC management the fortunes of the company were being steered in the right direction.

On 12 May 1942 it was announced that Sir Ralph Wedgwood, who had been appointed chairman of both ABPC and Union Cinemas Ltd. in September 1941, had resigned. No reason was given.

The new chairman of ABPC was to be A.G.Allen, senior partner in the firm of solicitors Allen & Overy, representing the interests of Mrs John Maxwell. He was also appointed a director of Union Cinemas, together with Dr E.G.M.Fletcher, another solicitor who was also a director of Warner Brothers whose interest he represented. The new chairman of Union Cinemas was to be P.A.Warter, a director of the British and

Foreign Wharf Co. Ltd., who was a son-in-law of Mrs Maxwell. The joint managing directors of both companies were to be Eric Lightfoot and Max Milder, the latter also being a director of Warner Brothers. At this point it should be noted that Mrs Maxwell had inherited the bulk of her husband's shareholdings and thus effective control of his entertainment empire. After payment of death duties, new management arrangements were clearly necessary and, of several bids received from interested parties, that from Warner Brothers was the largest and therefore the successful one.

Towards the end of June it was announced that the trading profit of Union Cinemas Ltd. in 1941 amounted to no less than £591,746 - a huge improvement over the previous year. A provision of £250,000 was made for taxation, together with a transfer of £150,000 to a newly-formed company reserve. It was judged unnecessary to make a further provision for Excess Profits Tax as sufficient had been set aside previously to more than cover this requirement, hence the establishment of a reserve to be available against future contingencies. The reserve for taxation had been substantially increased, as had the reserve for depreciation and amortisation. The bank overdraft had also been considerably reduced, reflecting improved business during the year.

At the Annual General Meeting of Union Cinemas Ltd. held on Wednesday 1 July 1942 at the Regal, Marble Arch, the chairman Mr P.A.Warter advised shareholders that ABPC would be making an offer for the ordinary shares of the company not already held by them. The terms were not announced at the meeting itself, but followed in a statement released the next day. Holders of the outstanding shares would be offered 2s.6d. for each 5s.0d. share, as against the market price of 2s.1½d. The issued ordinary capital was £1,950,213, of which ABPC already owned 70%; purchase of the remaining 30% would require £292,531.

The statement pointed out that there was little prospect of ordinary shareholders receiving any return in the form of dividends and that in terms of control and management it would make for greater efficiency if the whole of the ordinary shares were owned by ABPC. Again, because of the large number of small shareholders involved, the administrative costs would obviously be considerably reduced.

Evidently this proposal paid off. By the end of July, ABPC had acquired 88% of the shares and the offer to purchase the remainder was left open. In November, notice was given that these would be acquired

127

compulsorily under provisions in the Companies Act of 1929. Any applications to oppose this step had to be lodged before 4 December, but by now the matter had become somewhat academic.

As regards the preference shares, the stock market reaction to all this was a continued rise in their prices: the First Preference rose to 18s.6d. and the Second Preference to 17s.0d. at once, with further increases to follow in the course of the year. Eventually they would reach par value.

Mention has been made earlier of the purchase by John Maxwell in 1936 of a large holding of Gaumont-British "B" shares which entitled him to a 5-year option on acquiring 51% of the "A" shares in Metropolitan & Bradford Trust Ltd. which held the controlling shares in Gaumont-British. Though not strictly relevant to our story, it is worth recording that in September 1942 the Rank Organisation bought back these shares (250,000 "B" non-voting Ordinary) as the option had lapsed and there was little point in ABPC retaining them. The effect was to remove any basis for the eventual control of Gaumont-British which Maxwell presumably had in mind prior to the opportunity presented to him to acquire control of Union Cinemas in the following year.

In 1943 continued interest in buying the preference shares in due course resulted in their market prices recovering to par value, bringing with it the expectation that the company would take action to fund the dividend arrears and then to resume normal payments. The arrears, going back to 1937, amounted to 6s.0d. per share.

Because of the large bank overdraft - stated to be £646,422 at the end of 1942 - and the continued existence of the suspense account, the directors felt unable to payout the arrears in the form of cash. Instead, they announced an issue of £197,222 in redeemable income certificates at 5% to be allotted to preference shareholders on the basis of 3s.0d. for each share held. If this scheme was approved, payment of dividends would be resumed from 1 April 1943. Shareholders who did not wish to retain the income certificates would be given the opportunity to sell them at £99 per cent through the company's brokers for a limited period only.

The effect of the announcement was actually a further rise in the preference share prices: the 1st Preference by 1s.6d. to 22s.6d. and the Second Preference by 6d. to 20s.6d. There were smaller increases in the share prices of the parent company ABPC on the news of the measures being taken to clear the dividend arrears.

128

Accompanying the statement referred to above was the 1942 trading report. This showed that the trading profit for that year amounted to £423,511. The sum of £60,000 was taken for depreciation and amortisation, £100,000 for income tax, £100,000 for reserve and £4,834 as provision against war damage. Provision for the payment of preference share dividends for the three months to 31 December 1942 was also made. Then with the balance of £62,490 brought forward from that year, a total of £81,982 was available to be carried forward.

The chairman, P.A.Warter, was able to report that cinema earnings had been well up on the previous year, though Excess Profits Tax had affected trading profits to a considerable extent. It will be remembered that in 1941 it had not been necessary to make provision for this tax as more than sufficient funds to cover it had been set aside previously.

Having acquired ownership of the whole of the ordinary shares by the end of 1942, with the company trading profitably and the payment of dividends on the preference shares resumed, this may be taken as a suitable point at which to end our story. However, Union Cinemas continued to operate as a subsidiary company within the ABPC Group for several more years before being fully absorbed by it.

CHAPTER TWELVE

THE UNION CINEMA, KINGSTON

SOME PERSONAL RECOLLECTIONS

FIRST IMPRESSIONS

My first visit to the Regal, Kingston, took place soon after the cinema opened in 1932. At that time my family was living in the Epsom/Ashtead area of Surrey and I was a young lad at prep school. Indeed, one of the reasons for remembering that visit so well was that I had placed my school cap under my seat in the stalls and when the time came to leave I leant down to pick it up, only to find it no longer there! A few minutes spent scrabbling around failed to find it, so I decided that somebody must have kicked it into touch and that it had been well and truly lost. It was to be the first of several school caps to disappear over the ensuing years!

But a much more interesting reason to remember the visit was my first ever encounter with the cinema organ, in this case the celebrated 3-manual 12-unit Wurlitzer, played by none other than Reginald Foort himself. He introduced each item in that inimitable way of his which became so familiar to BBC listeners in later years, and I recall that one of the numbers he played that afternoon was the popular melody "Love is the sweetest thing."

I remember that the organ console was finished in white, with the inside of the horseshoe (containing the manuals, pistons and stopkeys) in a dark chocolate brown colour. I noted that the console was mounted on a lift with an unusually short travel, the "down" position

130

being at about the same level as the floor of the cinema, so that the top half remained in view above the rail of the orchestra pit. In the "up" position, the lift took the console to stage level.

Of the film programme itself I can remember absolutely nothing!

After that first visit to the Regal in 1932, I did not go there again for some years, the family having moved to Wandsworth Common. However, the Regal continued to feature "on the air" with broadcasts by Reginald New and Rex O'Grady at the Wurlitzer organ. My own cinema-going became more frequent in the ensuing years, but the organ did not figure very much, although an anonymous individual used to play the small 1927 Christie Unit Organ at the Picture House, Balham, in between the films. The console was in a fixed position in the pit, with the chamber located high up on pillars in a sort of transept to the right of the auditorium. On occasional visits to my grandmother's house in Clapham I would sometimes go to the Majestic, situated in the High Street, and there I used to hear the Compton organ. Many years later, I found out that this had been one of the first two instruments with 3 manuals and 6 units to be turned out by that builder, the other being installed at the Marlborough, Holloway. Each had been opened by Leslie James - Holloway on 14 April 1930 and Clapham the following week. So far as my visits to Clapham were concerned, the identity of the organist again remained unknown.

These represented my sole "live" encounters with cinema organs for quite a long time, but of course I listened to a good many BBC broadcasts as well. In that way I got to know all the great "stars" of that time - Maclean, Newman, Dixon, Porter-Brown, Bayco and so on, as well as Foort, of course. I remember listening to Robinson Cleaver's first broadcast from the Regal, Bexley Heath, in January 1936, and of course in October that year I listened to the Opening Broadcast of the brand new BBC Compton Theatre Organ. Each week, Radio Times contained details of forthcoming cinema organ broadcasts and quite frequently these would be supplemented by pictures of various organists seated at their instruments. Such broadcasts were immensely popular in those days. In due course there were published two series of articles about the "star" players, written by Leslie Barnard.

"HAROLD RAMSAY NOW BROADCASTING"
My interest in cinema organs increased rapidly with the advent of Union Cinemas. I had listened often enough to Harold Ramsay's Saturday afternoon broadcasts, originally from the Granada, Tooting,

and later from the Regal, Kingston, but what eventually led me to make another trip to Kingston was the announcement on 6 March 1937 that the broadcast that afternoon was coming from the Union, Kingston, even though Radio Times still listed it as the Regal. I listened to the broadcast and the distinctive voicing of the Regal Wurlitzer made it obvious that the same organ was being played as usual. Changes of cinema name were virtually unheard of in those days and I felt I just had to go down to Kingston and see for myself that the Union was indeed the Regal - that big cinema just across the road from Kingston railway station. I kept a close watch on Radio Times to see when the next broadcast would be taking place; sure enough, it duly appeared, scheduled for Saturday 27 March - from the Union, Kingston!

So, after an early lunch that Saturday, I duly caught a Kingston train from Clapham Junction which would deliver me to the cinema at about 2.30., in good time for the broadcast at 3.00. Even before I had bought my admission ticket I noticed a large sign mounted on an easel in the vestibule, which read "Harold Ramsay broadcasting today at 3.00", or words to that effect. Once seated, two surprises followed in quick succession. The first was that the film being shown came to an end after only ten minutes or so, whereupon the sounds of "Rhapsody in Blue" came from the organ and up came Harold Ramsay, smiling broadly and turning round to the audience, first to the right and then to the left, playing with his left hand only and using second touch. The second surprise was that the console looked quite different from the way I remembered it from my visit five years earlier. The casework was now painted gold with the name "Wurlitzer" picked out in red on either side, there was a different type of music desk, and there was an illuminated glass surround. I began to wonder if this was a different organ altogether... But the familiar sounds were still there.

Harold Ramsay started by chatting to the audience for about five minutes, describing the double opening which had taken place at the beginning of the week: the Ritz, Chatham, and the Ritz, Barnsley. He himself had been appearing all week at Chatham, so he had obviously had to return to Kingston specially to do the broadcast (Presumably Phil Park, who was billed to appear at Kingston, went down to Chatham on the Saturday). He then went on to say that he was going to rehearse us in the two numbers that we were to sing as part of the Popular Medley towards the end of the broadcast (Community singing was a regular feature of Harold Ramsay's programmes broadcast when there was an audience present). The first title was "There's a small hotel" but I cannot recall what the second was. I found out later that many cinema organists had some difficulty in persuading their audiences to sing, but Ramsay had no problems in that respect and certainly at Kingston there was good, lusty singing from the word go! Nevertheless, he took us through each number a couple of times, suddenly waving at us to stop as the red light started flashing to indicate that we were going "on air" and reverting to his signature tune, "Rhapsody in Blue."

The actual broadcast lasted thirty minutes and was full of interest, starting with the "Washington Post" march by Sousa. This was followed by a selection of songs by Horatio Nicholls, the very famous "Dinah" and one of Ramsay's own compositions, "This Lovely Rose." Finally there came the "Popular Melodies" - five numbers in all, of which the audience sang the second and fourth, Ramsay bringing us in with a very professional sweep of the arm each time.

The day's proceedings were not yet over: the main feature film followed the broadcast, and then came a stage show with four different variety acts, the final one of course featuring the "top of the bill" artiste, who turned out to be the great Teddy Brown, xylophonist and drummer. In spite of his enormous girth, Brown seemed to be as light as a feather on his feet, stepping all around the xylophone while playing - and never missing a note! Then he moved over to his drum kit and having performed a remarkable solo on the drums joined Harold Ramsay (who had been accompanying the stage show throughout) in an exhilarating rendition of "Tiger Rag." All in all, it had been a truly memorable afternoon!

"Tiger Rag" was the concluding number in another broadcast I attended: this was one of the evening transmissions which became quite frequent during 1937, on 24 June at 7.30 . As I recall, this one overran slightly. The red light went out and Ramsay started the lift on its downward path whilst still playing the final chorus; having ended it, he did not bother to play his signature tune.

"RADIO RODEO"
Following the success of the earlier variety broadcasts from the stage of the Union, Kingston, including the "Radio Round-Up" show transmitted in March, the first of the regular monthly "Radio Rodeos" went out on the air on 6 May 1937. For the actual broadcast itself an expensive "top of the bill" artiste was engaged, in this instance the great comedian George Robey, but for the remainder of the week the show was presented as part of the normal Kingston programme. I was not

present on the night of the broadcast but was there on one of the other evenings - I am not sure which. Harold Ramsay was very much in charge, acting as compére and playing the organ for the "Rodeo March" signature tune, for which he had composed the music and Phil Park had written the lyric. Sidney Torch then took over at the organ, with Phil Park on piano; I was disappointed that Robinson Cleaver was missing from the scene.

The show was very enjoyable, being a great deal more lavish than most Cine-Variety presentations of the period. Gypsy Nina and the Ladies Accordion Band were quite spectacular and Randolph Sutton - "Britain's Premier Light Comedian" - gave a wonderful performance. There were two contrasting comedy double acts: Clapham & Dwyer and Stanford & McNaughton. The popular Carlyle Cousins were also featured. Later on in the evening, after the main film had been shown, came a real bonus: a concert performance of Gershwin's "Rhapsody in Blue" performed by Harold Ramsay at the organ and Sidney Torch and Phil Park at two grand pianos. After such a big stage show, one had certainly not been expecting this, which made it all the more memorable.

The next "Radio Rodeo" I attended was the August edition and on this occasion I was actually present for the evening of the broadcast. The "top of the bill" artiste on this occasion was none other than Cicely Courtneidge, famous as a stage and film actress as well as a comedienne regularly appearing on radio. Others included the oddly eccentric comedian Claude Dampier with his partner Billy Carlyle, Billy Costello (the voice of Popeye the Sailor in the popular cartoons), double act Rusty & Shine, and The Four Aces who were close harmony singers. Needless to say, I was delighted to see that Robinson Cleaver was present on this occasion, together with Messrs. Ramsay, Torch and Park. The organ and two pianos were complemented by a percussionist.

The actual broadcast was scheduled to commence at 8.35 pm, but the film preceding it finished about half an hour earlier. I noticed that before this a temporary screen was dropped down near the front of the stage so that preparations could be made behind it. As the film ended, the curtain closed in front of this screen. The house lights went up and there was a short interval during which members of the audience could make themselves comfortable and get settled. Then the organ console rose on its lift to stage level, being operated by remote control; this seemed to me to demonstrate that the organ was central to the whole show. The curtains then opened to reveal the familiar ranch setting which had been adopted for the "Radio Rodeo" shows, with "cowboys"

134

sitting around to give added realism. A few moments later Harold Ramsay emerged from the wings on the right hand side of the stage, wearing a white suit, navy blue shirt and a blue and white striped tie and carrying a clip-board, and made his way down to the waiting microphone at the front of the gangway placed over the orchestra pit at the side of the console. After a few introductory remarks and telling the audience a little about what would be happening, he welcomed the other organists one by one - starting with Robinson Cleaver who entered from the opposite side of the stage, walked down the gangway on the other side of the console and took his place at the organ. Sidney Torch also entered from that side and stepped down to the grand piano in the pit; Phil Park then appeared from the wings on the right and stepped down to a second grand piano. All three wore dinner suits and black bow ties.

There followed rehearsal of the audience in singing the words of the "Rodeo March" and one or two other numbers, including "Home on the Range" which had become a firm favourite and virtually an anthem at the Union, Kingston, in those days. Robinson Cleaver played the organ during this session and also played for the show itself during the broadcast. However, for the actual opening, Harold Ramsay' signature tune "Rhapsody in Blue" was to be played and shortly before the "on the air" red light began to flash, it was Cleaver who started to play it. But then came a clever switch, with Ramsay placing his hands over Cleaver's and taking over, sliding onto the bench from one side as Cleaver slid off from the other, with no break in the music. Thus Ramsay played as the broadcast began and he continued for the "Rodeo March." After that, Cleaver replaced Ramsay at the console and the latter resumed the role of compère for the rest of the show.

The various artistes were presented and performed their acts with distinction. Although this was a show designed for broadcasting, they nevertheless wore appropriate costume: for example, Billy Costello was in his "Popeye the sailor" outfit - complete with bulging fore-arms! Claude Dampier appeared in gum boots, old-fashioned bathing costume, Sou'wester hat and a fur, his sketch involving laboured explanations for donning such garb. He made numerous references to "my friend Mrs Gibson" - a fictitious character who figured in all his sketches and who appeared to be the cause of so many of his odd escapades. Cicely Courtneidge in evening dress performed some of her best-known routines, including the tongue-twisting "Two dozen double-damask dinner napkins" which she was trying to order on the telephone and the delightful monologue in which she was standing in the crowd as the royal procession went by and the King smiled directly at her. It may sound like mundane stuff now, but she put it over with style and panache and even a touch of drama.

When the broadcast was finished and the red light was out, Harold Ramsay thanked the audience for their participation in the show and told them that everything had gone over very well. The main curtains were drawn again for a short interval, after which the main feature film of the evening began - again using the temporary screen at the front of the stage until the latter had been cleared and the permanent screen could be employed again.

Towards the end of the Union period a special club was started with the object of providing a Sunday morning audience for the somewhat similar "Radio Parade" shows which were recorded for transmission from the commercial station Radio Normandy. However, not being resident in the Kingston area in those days I did not bother to join, though I did listen in to some of the actual broadcasts. Later on, after ABC had assumed control, the venue changed from the Union, Kingston, to the Regal, Walham Green.

EPILOGUE

I have often thought that it must have been largely due to the impact of the musical and live entertainment activities at this wonderful cinema, together with broadcasts by a large number of well-known cinema organists over a long period, that in ABC days it continued as the base for that company's Musical Directors. These included Harold Coombs, officially referred to as "Chief Organist", for some years until his appointment as the Borough Organist of Bournemouth following the untimely death of Percy Whitlock. During his time at Kingston he gave many broadcasts on the organ and after his departure the broadcasts continued, being given by several different organists including Nelson Elms, Andrew Fenner, Frank Newman, Wilson Oliphant, Reginald New, Arthur Lord, Molly Forbes and Hubert Selby.

The next appointment as Musical Director went to Joseph Seal who had been a member of the Union team and after the customary touring had settled as resident organist at the Ritz, Belfast, where he remained for some fourteen years, broadcasting frequently.

Joseph Seal arrived at Kingston in 1951 and remained there until the very end. In due course, he became Controller of Entertainment as well, live stage shows being produced on special occasions from time to time around the ABC circuit. With his wife and daughter he took up residence in nearby New Malden. I myself was working in Kingston by then and also moved to New Malden in 1954, coming to know the Seal family well as time went by. It struck me as unfortunate that the Kingston organ was no longer featured in the cinema, though Joseph Seal continued to use it for broadcasts and recordings. I was invited to be present during a number of broadcasts and, not owning a car in those days, was grateful to be offered a lift home after the late night transmissions! He very kindly consented to perform at the inaugural meeting of the Cinema Organ Society at the Ritz, Richmond, on 11 January 1953 and readily gave permission for subsequent meetings to be held at many of the ABC houses, including Kingston and other cinemas which had been either acquired or newly built by Union. Although the policy of inviting other organists to broadcast from Kingston had been discontinued, according to Radio Times, Reginald Porter-Brown did broadcast from the Regal on 11 December 1959.

These recollections would not be complete without a mention of Clifford Birchall, a talented organist who was a member of the ABC touring team and had the Regal, Kingston, as his base theatre for a few years from 1950. I remember him telling me that his "party piece" was playing Sousa's "Stars and Stripes" March complete with the piccolo part thrown in for good measure: apparently he had discussed this with Reginald Foort who had said that it couldn't be done, whereupon he proceeded to perform it there and then! He did the same for me one morning at the Regal, and I must say it was most effectively played, using second touch in the left hand to perform the main tune and its accompaniment and using the right hand for the piccolo. Quite a feat, really, to keep everything going together!

It was some time in the 1950s that I heard a most remarkable account of the bombing which the Regal suffered in October 1940. I cannot remember for sure who it was who told me, but I think it could well have been Joe Quick, the Chief Projectionist, who had been at the Regal for many years including the whole of the Union period. Apparently there was a house rule that the safety curtain should be lowered every night after the cinema closed, the thinking being that in the event of a bomb incident the building would be effectively divided in two, thereby confining the damage to the one half only. It seems that on the night the bomb actually fell, by an oversight the safety curtain had not been lowered and the blast from the explosion at the stage end travelled over a wider area and in doing so became less concentrated. As it was, the shutters of the scenery dock door were blown out, allowing much of the blast to disperse outside in the street. Had the safety curtain been down, it was believed that one or more of the walls surrounding the stage would have been demolished and the roof would have come down as well - producing far more serious damage than actually occurred! As it was, damage to the interior was widespread and a good deal of repair work and replacement had to be undertaken in order for the cinema to be reopened.

The Wurlitzer organ at Kingston was finally removed in October 1972 but happily found a new home at the Musical Museum in Brentford, where it continues in use to this day, in concerts featuring guest organists as well as the Museum's own resident, Richard Cole. It can also be played without an organist being present, by means of the remarkable automatic player mechanism whereby the instrument is operated from perforated paper rolls cut many years ago by Jesse Crawford and other pioneer American cinema organists.

Today, the Kingston cinema, in its time known as the Regal, Union, Regal again, ABC, Cannon, and - latterly in its guise as a bingo hall - Coral Social Club and Gala Club, still stands there on the corner of Richmond Road and Canbury Park Road. For me, it is still the Regal and every time I pass it - which I do quite often - I remember those wonderful days when so many of our most famous stars appeared on its stage and so many of our greatest cinema organists were featured at its Mighty Wurlitzer! Halcyon days indeed and, compared with the fare on offer from the multiplex movie-houses of the 1990s, the entertainment and showmanship regularly provided by cinemas like the Regal in those golden years represented truly incredible value for money.

CHAPTER THIRTEEN

HAROLD RAMSAY THE LATER YEARS

I feel that Harold Ramsay held such an important and central position in Union Cinemas during the Company's "Golden Years" that our story would not be complete without some reference to his activities in the world of entertainment in the years that followed.

Having been introduced to a completely new audience through the "Radio Rodeo" and "Radio Parade" variety shows, Harold Ramsay had the idea to capitalise on this by going out on a tour of the country's leading music halls and variety theatres with a stage act. At first he appeared as a solo performer playing a Hammond/Lafleur electronic organ. Some time after the outbreak of war in 1939 there were requests to include vocal numbers, so he expanded the show to include a girls' choir known as "The Eight Lovely Ladies", touring as before but also broadcasting from time to time. As a contribution to boosting wartime morale the group also appeared in shows for the Forces and at various fund-raising events such as "Warship Week" and so on. The standard of singing was particularly high and several of the girls went on to achieve successful careers as soloists, notably Victoria Sladen who later became a famous operatic soprano.

In 1942 Harold Ramsay and his wife Cherrie Cooper devised a new organ and vocal act which again toured successfully over a long period. Occasionally, as engagements permitted, he would break away and renew his connections with the cinema organ, making guest appearances at well-known venues. For example, the week commencing 8 June 1942 found him at the Granada, Clapham Junction, where I was lucky enough to catch him: he was in tremendous form and obviously enjoying himself immensely, as was his audience - the community singing was as lusty and as enthusiastic as I remembered it being at Kingston in the old days.

In 1945 Harold Ramsay was initiated into the Grand Order of Water Rats for his services to variety - surely a unique honour for a cinema organist. Bud Flanagan was King Rat at the time and there was some publicity for a forthcoming "world tour" by the two of them. However, I have been unable to find any evidence that this actually took place. In October 1946 it was announced that Harold Ramsay had been engaged once again as resident organist at the Granada, Tooting, for an indefinite period. Jack Courtnay, writing in the trade press, went to hear the opening performance, wondering how it would go after such a lengthy absence, but reported that he need not have worried: "Let me say right away that my anxiety was groundless - here is a showman who, if anything, has gained assurance from his holiday from the cinema and rarely have I heard a solo listened to so intently, or as much appreciated, as was Harold's contrarious medley." Among the items performed were "I got rhythm," "Night and day," "Sleepy lagoon" and "Annie Laurie."

Broadcasts, however, were relatively few and far between during this period. It does seem a little odd that, at a time when considerable numbers of cinema organ broadcasts were taking place, often given by organists new to the air waves and often played on organs equally new, that such a distinguished performer should be so seldom featured. It may be that "new management" was at work! Of course, in common with other artistes, Harold Ramsay did have his detractors and his particular style of playing did not appeal to everyone. The same could probably be said of some other organists who had been regular broadcasters before the war but who now appeared to be excluded. One of these was Horace Finch of the Empress Ballroom, Blackpool, almost certainly the most senior member of the Blackpool team, having been with that company since 1926 and organist at the Empress Ballroom from the opening of its Wurlitzer organ in April 1935. He commenced regular broadcasts a few months later. All sorts of possible reasons were suggested for his exclusion from broadcasting for several years after the war, but he did eventually resume in the late 1950s. The fact remains that despite everything organists such as these continued to enjoy great popularity with the audiences for whom they played.

In time, however, Harold Ramsay evidently decided that after eighteen years in this country it was time for him to return to Canada - which he did in 1950. Before leaving these shores, it worth recording that he was founder-conductor of the Merton and Morden Choral Society numbering some 200 voices, with whom he gave the European premiere of the Coopersmith edition of Handel's "Messiah." He was also made President of the Merton and Morden Children's Camping Association.

Back in Calgary once again, Harold Ramsay was appointed Master of the Music at the Wesley United Church and joined the teaching staff of the Mount Royal Junior College. Not long afterwards he became Director of the Conservatory of Music at Mount Royal College. In 1953 I had some correspondence with him, in the course of which he made reference to other organists who had moved to Canada, including of course the great Quentin Maclean. Frederick Geoghegan, formerly at All Souls, Langham Place, had actually joined the staff at the Conservatory. Apparently they had around 700 students there, so it was a flourishing institution at that time! Harold Ramsay himself continued to conduct annual performances of the "Messiah" and when the Southern Alberta Jubilee Auditorium was opened in 1957 he was able to combine the Wesley Choir with the Calgary Choral Society (of which he had been conductor since its inception in 1952) and transfer the performances to the new venue.

After retirement, Harold Ramsay continued to teach for some years until eventually he suffered a stroke and was obliged to give up. With his wife Cherrie he moved to Salmon Arm, British Columbia, where he ended his days some five years later: he died on 28 January 1976 aged 75 years. A memorial service was held at the Wesley United Church in Calgary on 2 February 1976. I wrote to his widow and was delighted to receive a most charming hand-written reply by return.

Harold Ramsay and his wife did however visit this country once again in 1973 when they were the guests of Cecil Bernstein. For us enthusiasts the highlight of the visit was undoubtedly the concert they gave at the Granada, Tooting, on 17 June: even with minimal advance publicity that huge cinema saw what must have been one of the largest audiences ever seen at an organ presentation. It was a truly memorable occasion and all of us who were there felt greatly privileged to have been present. Robin Richmond - another veteran who did so much for the cinema organ with his Radio 2 broadcasts of "The Organist Entertains" - acted as Master of Ceremonies and something of a party atmosphere quickly developed. Former Union organists Neville Meale and Ray Baines were also present, the latter paying handsome tribute to Harold Ramsay as the one who had given him his first chance as a cinema organist.

Ramsay played a wide variety of pieces and showed that he had lost none of his old skills. A series of his own compositions led to Robin Richmond suggesting that Cherrie should sing some of them, which she did to such effect as to stop the show! Between the various items there was quite a lot of chat, in the course of which some interesting anecdotes and snippets of information came out, adding to the general feeling of nostalgia which characterised this concert. It was an occasion that all of us who were present will never forget.

Finally, mention may also be made of the honorary Fellowship of Trinity College, London, which was conferred on Harold Ramsay in 1952. He had been a Fellow of the American National Association of Teachers of Singing and a President of the Calgary branch of the Royal Canadian College of Organists - doubtless these would have been honorary positions as well. It would probably be fair to say that - notwithstanding all the earlier successes he had enjoyed - it was in these later years that Harold Ramsay really found himself. One might add that another distinguished cinema organist (who had spent part of his career with Union Cinemas) truly found himself in later years when he began a new career in the role of composer, arranger and conductor of light music: Sidney Torch, who for many years was responsible for "Friday Night is Music Night" on BBC Radio Two.

APPENDIX ONE

REGAL, KINGSTON ON THAMES FEBRUARY 1932.

The following is an extract from the Souvenir Programme published to mark the opening ceremony of the Regal Cinema in February 1932.

The Theatre - Then and Now.

On the inauguration of the new "Regal" Cinema, it is interesting to recall that this latest example of modern architecture - built by Mr. James Watt, stands upon the site of the "Central" Palace, erected by him in 1909 - Kingston's first "picture-house." Neither of these Theatres might ever have been built had Edward Muybridge not been born (also in Kingston) in 1830. Muybridge was a mechanical genius with a penchant for photography. He invented the "zoopraxiscope" in 1881 - a photographic-camera designed for the specific purpose of repro- ducing the actions of animals in motion. His efforts led the way to the evolving of the cinematograph which was the immediate result of Dr. Marey's invention of the celluloid roll-film in 1890. In the short period of four decades, the motion picture has been improved and developed to such an extra-ordinary pitch of perfection - for not only is light photographed, but the sound of the Talkies is also reproduced by the photo-electric cell from graduated shadows formed on the edge of the films by means of the camera. And what a change has been effected in the Cinema Theatres! It is only a few years since these were compara- tively inefficient, uncomfortable and badly designed.

Today

Today the latest developments in science and engineering-structural, electrical and acoustical - combined with the specialist knowledge of

143

the Architect - give us Cinemas which in name and in fact can only be described as Regal.

Constructed throughout of fire-resisting materials, brick, steel and concrete - the new "Regal" has taken over a year to build. In its erection some 200 local men have found employment. Standing upon an acre of ground the Theatre accommodates 3,000 people with one balcony. There is a full-sized stage complete with fireproof curtain, grid, counterweights, dressing rooms and all the accessories, electrical and mechanical, necessary for the production of stage plays and vaudeville.

Owing to the shape of the Site, the Theatre has its axis parallel to the Richmond Road. This arrangement necessitated the entrance being at the end of the facade - immediately opposite the Railway Station.

Architectural Dignity

There is a dignity about some of the modern architecture of today which is rarely exemplified in cinema buildings, but in the case of the "Regal," with its soft-toned brickwork handled in plain masses contrasting with white fluted and carved stonework in simple lines, the Directors feel-that the Richmond Road has been enriched. Designed by Mr. Robert Cromie, F.R.I.B.A., a leading specialist in theatre-work, the new "Regal" is the last word in efficiency. The sight-lines from every seat to the stage are perfect. There are no columns to obstruct the view.

Accessibility to every part, wide gangways and an abundance of exits are characteristic, The balcony is built upon the cantilever principle - of British steel. Rolled-steel raking joists supported upon a steel-plate girder 90 ft. long, 8 ft. deep, and weighing 40 tons, carry the balcony tiers. A notable feature of the balcony is its accessibility - only a short staircase linking it to the entrance floor.

The Structure

The structure of the "Regal" Theatre is completely steel-framed and consists, in addition to the Theatre proper, of a four-storied building containing boiler house, three floors of dressing rooms and accommodation for the ventilating and heating plant.

The main entrance hall is 60 ft. long and 30 ft. wide; the tea room immediately above the entrance hall, is 70 ft. long and 46 ft. extreme width.

144

UNION CINEMAS
WORLD'S LARGEST INDEPENDENT CIRCUIT

THURSDAY NEXT
GRAND CORONATION
GALA OPENING
OF
UNION CINEMAS RITZ
ALDERSHOT

CORONATION
SPEECH
OF
H.M. THE KING
WILL BE RELAYED AT
ALL
UNION CINEMAS
THROUGHOUT THE
BRITISH ISLES

UNION CINEMAS

Sensational Announcement!

UNION CINEMAS
STAGE · CHATHAM **RITZ** PHONE 3681 · STAGE

MON · NEXT
HAROLD RAMSAY
PRESENTS
UNION CINEMAS
GREAT B·B·C BROADCAST SHOW
'RADIO RODEO'

WITH
THE RENOWNED B·B·C KOLOURED KOMEDY KINGS
SCOTT & WHALEY

IRENE PRICE | THE KRAKAJAX
BRITAINS SHIRLEY TEMPLE | THE FAMOUS B·B·C RECORDING STARS

THE 8 STEP SISTERS THE ORIGINAL B·B·C FAVOURITES

THE 2 NEW YORKERS | FRED HUDSON
COMEDY & CLEVERNESS | THE BRILLIANT NEW B·B·C STAR

AND
HAROLD RAMSAY
"UNION CINEMAS ACE ORGANIST OF THE AIR"
CONTINUITY BY PHIL PARK | PRODUCED BY LEON POLLOCK

ON THE SCREEN

CAPT DRUMMOND RETURNS IN A WHIRL
OF THRILLS & ADVENTURE !

BULLDOG DRUMMOND ESCAPES U.
WITH
SIR GUY STANDING
RAY MILLAND · HEATHER ANGEL

UNION CINEMAS RITZ CAFE | UNION CINEMAS CHUMS CLUB | SUNDAY · OCT 3RD
OPEN TO THE PUBLIC DAILY | EVERY SAT at 10 a.m. CHILDREN 3½ 6ᵈ | IF YOU COULD ONLY COOK WITH
FROM 2 p.m. 10·30 p.m. SUN. 3 - 10 p.m. | ADULTS 6ᵈ OCT 2. SHIRLEY TEMPLE | JEAN ARTHUR, HERBERT MARSHALL
 | in POLYTITE in WASHINGTON. NEW | ALSO. BLACKMAILER WITH

HORSHAM GOES CRAZY
TERRIFIC CUT IN PRICES
FAMOUS VARIETY ACTS on STAGES
PERSONAL APPEARANCE OF
HAROLD RAMSAY
ENGLAND'S LEADING B.B.C. BROADCASTING ARTISTE
SPECIAL ARRANGEMENT WITH THE STUDIOS
ALL THE BIG FILMS HAVE BEEN BOOKED FOR PRESENTATION

MON. NEXT

HE STANDS ALONE AS THE GREATEST ENTERTAINER OF MODERN TIMES —

RITZ PHONE 000.

PERSONAL APPEARANCE of

CHARLIE CHAPLIN
MODERN TIMES
in PAULETTE GODDARD

HAROLD RAMSAY
IN A NEW & NOVEL ORGAN PRESENTATION
LISTEN TO THE SPECIAL HAROLD RAMSAY B.B.C. BROADCASTS ON OCT. 2 AT 6.25 AND OCT. 3 AT 9.40 P.M.

SHIRLEY TEMPLE
CAPTAIN JANUARY

GRACIE FIELDS
in QUEEN OF HEARTS

MUTINY on the BOUNTY
CHARLES LAUGHTON-CLARK GABLE

JESSIE MATTHEWS
in IT'S LOVE AGAIN

TALE of TWO CITIES
RONALD COLMAN-ELIZABETH ALLAN

FREDDIE BARTHOLOMEW
in Little LORD FAUNTLEROY

MADELEINE CARROLL
in SECRET AGENT

MYRNA LOY
CLARK GABLE & JEAN HARLOW
in WIFE - SECRETARY

RONALD COLMAN
CLAUDETTE COLBERT
in UNDER TWO FLAGS

UNION CINEMA Co.
REGAL
KINGSTON · PHONE 6325-6
MON NEXT

Definitely — **THE GREATEST STAGE SCREEN AND ORGAN PRESENTATION SEEN IN KINGSTON THIS YEAR!**

STAGE
THE GREATEST NOVELTY IN VARIETY TO-DAY
ARCHIE and his **JUVENILE BAND**
THE YOUNGEST BAND IN THE WORLD

JACK TRACY & INGA ANDERSON
THE SAP AND THE SWELL DAME

THE **FOUR RICHLEYS**
SENSATIONAL ACROBATS

JOHNNY NIT THE WORLD'S GREATEST TAP DANCER

FIRST TIME IN KINGSTON!
THE INTERNATIONAL BROADCASTING AND RECORDING "STAR"
SIDNEY TORCH
AT THE REGAL ORGAN

SCREEN
KARLOFF IN
THE MAN WHO CHANGED HIS MIND
WITH **ANNA LEE**
ALSO
WANTED MEN WITH ROY MASON RUSSELL HOPTON

SUN. NOV. 15. NEXT TIME WE LIVE & Mr COHEN TAKES A WALK

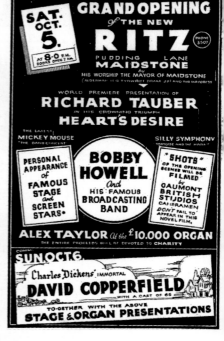

SAT. OCT. 5.
AT 8·0 P.M.
DOORS OPEN 7 P.M.

GRAND OPENING
of **THE NEW**
RITZ PHONE 3507.
PUDDING LANE
MAIDSTONE
by
HIS WORSHIP THE MAYOR OF MAIDSTONE
(ALDERMAN H.G. TYRWHITT DRAKE J.P.) AND THE MAYORESS

WORLD PREMIERE PRESENTATION OF
RICHARD TAUBER
IN HIS CROWNING TRIUMPH
HEART'S DESIRE

THE LATEST
MICKEY MOUSE
"THE BAND CONCERT"

SILLY SYMPHONY
TORTOISE AND THE HARE

PERSONAL APPEARANCE OF FAMOUS STAGE and SCREEN STARS

BOBBY HOWELL
And HIS FAMOUS BROADCASTING BAND

"SHOTS"
OF THE OPENING SCENE WILL BE **FILMED**
by GAUMONT BRITISH STUDIOS CAMERAMEN
DON'T FAIL TO APPEAR IN THIS NOVEL FILM.

ALEX TAYLOR At the £10,000 ORGAN
THE ENTIRE PROCEEDS WILL BE DEVOTED TO CHARITY

COMM.
SUN. OCT. 6.
Charles Dickens' IMMORTAL
DAVID COPPERFIELD
WITH A CAST OF 65

TO-GETHER WITH THE ABOVE
STAGE & ORGAN PRESENTATIONS

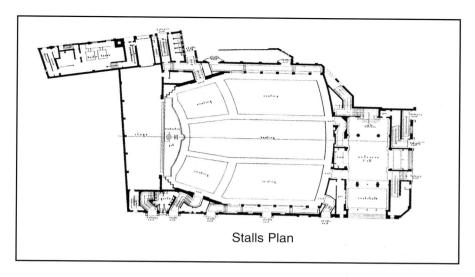

Stalls Plan

Adjacent to the tea room are commodious kitchens, staff rooms and stores. Above portion of the tea room, public toilets and offices are arranged. Immediately above these, the generator chamber and further public toilets are located.

One storey higher the projection chamber with secondary lighting, battery, re-wind, non-synchronous and repair rooms, together with the Electricians' Store, are arranged.

The planning, with the main entrance on the Upper Richmond Road facade and the balcony and tea room exits on the Canbury Park Road elevation, has resulted in a particularly convenient arrangement of the public and domestic accommodation immediately over the entrance hall.

The stalls floor is 160 ft. long on the axis line of the Theatre and 144 ft. wide.

The stage is 120 ft. long and of an average width of 25 ft.

The proscenium opening is 50 ft. wide and 30 ft. high.

The balcony is 75 ft. deep on the axis line of the Theatre from the fascia to the wall bounding the back promenade and its width is 144 ft.

The stage is equipped, not only for pictures, but for presentation of elaborate theatrical productions, being furnished with a steel grid 58 ft. above stage level, fitted with full counter-weight system.

145

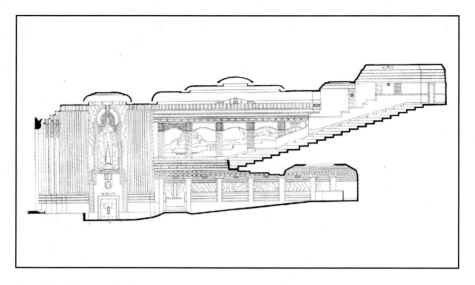

In the splayed flanks each side of the proscenium opening accommodation is provided, on four floors, for Stage Manager, public toilets,
orchestra room and music stores.

The whole of the foundations for the structural columns are of reinforced concrete, no steel grillages being used.

The stalls floor is of concrete laid direct upon formation and covered
with boarding on inset wood fillets.

The balcony with a cantilever overhanging span of 18 ft. is carried by
one balcony main girder 8 ft. deep and 20 in. wide, weighing 30 tons,
and two wing girders, which support eleven cantilever rakers.

The main roof over the auditorium is carried by nine steel-framed roof
girders varying in depth from 7 ft. to 14 ft., and in span from 72 ft. to
144 ft.

The roof girder immediately in advance of the proscenium wall is
specially designed to take the organ chamber, and the volume of sound
from the organ enters the auditorium through an ornamental grille
over the proscenium arch.

The rearmost of the roof girders carries a flat portion of the roof and
ceiling over the back of the balcony 30 ft. in width. The floors
throughout are of reinforced concrete construction.

146

The steelwork was designed by S. W. Budd, A.M.Inst.C.E., 68, Victoria Street, Westminster, London, S.W.1, and supplied and erected by Messrs. Braithwaite & Co., Ltd., of London and West Bromwich.

The Electrical Work
The whole of the Electrical equipment of the Building has been carried out by Mr. E. E. Dyne, E.C.A., of 247, Bromley Road, S.E.6, who is to be congratulated upon the excellent work and craftsmanship that has been put into this wonderful cinema. The organisation of his staff has enabled the apparatus to be installed without a single hitch, due to the careful co-operation with all other trades engaged in the building and his quick response to the requirements of the Consulting Engineer, Mr. A. Champion, who has chosen the whole of the electrical apparatus, consisting of the best the manufacturers of this country can produce.

Projection
The Projection chamber with its transformer and battery rooms, dimmers and controls, is situated at the rear, and entirely outside the public part of the building - the projection ports are glazed with fire-resisting glass in smoke-proof frames, and are fitted with automatic fire-proof shutters. Over a thousand pounds has been spent in eliminating any possible risk of fire.

The stage safety curtain of steel and asbestos is electrically controlled. It descends in 15 seconds at the touch of a button, and its seven tons weight are raised by a 10 h.p. electric motor.

Another form of electric hoist is used for raising the Organ console. Situated in the centre of the Orchestra well, the Organist plays a four-manual £10,000 Wurlitzer Organ housed in a special chamber in the roof. This chamber which is kept at a temperature of 65 to 68 deg. by thermostatically operated electric heaters, is designed with a stream-lined section to project the sound to the rear of the stalls and balcony.

Decoration
The auditorium decoration deserves comment. To avoid the common-place early Victorian decoration, and at the same time not to enter into the sphere of the ultra-modern or debased "jazz," requires special knowledge, taste and consummate skill. It is one thing to design on paper. It is another to draw the fibrous-plasterwork to scale, and then to decide on the colourings when the building is literally a forest of scaffolding and improperly illuminated. The Directors feel that their Architect has achieved an interior which is peculiarly distinctive and

refined, and except ionally pleasing in its "atmospheric" spaciousness. The opposing of the straight verticality of the walls with the curvilinear horizontality of the moulded ceilings has endowed the interior with an effect which must be seen to be appreciated. Pale green, dull gold and lacquered silver tones have been employed in conjunction with black and the varied lighting effects from the cornices.

A Country Garden

In the Entrance Hall the floor has been utilised for decoration - the mosaic design being based upon the lines of a formal garden with a lily-pond is just another touch of the originality which characterises the scheme throughout - while the Cafe over- is decorated in sunny colours for daylight as well as electric illumination. Its floor is of polished oak for dancing. At the end of the Cafe is a spacious "all electric" kitchen with the latest cookers and refrigerators, under the management of a capable restaurateur.

The heating and ventilation is on the now famous "plenum" or forced air-conditioning principle - the plant being capable of changing the whole of the atmosphere in the hall completely every fifteen minutes. The air is brought in by enormous fans, cleansed by being forced through water in spray-chambers, warmed by heating batteries, dried to the correct degree of humidity and delivered at the rate of two feet per second to every part of the Theatre - whence it is automatically extracted by super-silent fans.

The air is actually more healthy inside the Theatre than it is outside in the street!

It is impossible to describe all the multitudinous details which must be assembled in the construction and organisation of a modern super cinema - but the Directors hope, that having expended £150,000 in its erection and equipment, Kingston will be proud of its "Regal."

The Directors wish to acknowledge the services of Mr. Robert Cromie, F.RI.B.A., an eminent Theatre Architect, whose great ambition, viz., to raise cinema-architecture to the front rank, is rapidly being achieved; of Mr. S. W. Budd, A.M.I.C.E., Consulting Structural Engineer; Mr. A. Champion, Consulting Electrical Engineer, Mr. E. Dyne, for the wonderful electric installation; and finally Mr. W. Saunders, Foreman and his men.

148

The Policy

This latest addition to the Super-Cinema attractions now being erected in the London area will immediately recommend itself to the amusement-goers of Kingston and district. Standing, as it does, on a corner site adjoining Kingston Railway and Omnibus Stations, in an area which is thickly populated, it is a credit to the Directors of this palatial establishment that they have selected such a fine, commanding position for the erection of what will undoubtedly be one of the most popular rendezvous for local and distant residents.

No effort or expense has been spared to make the "Regal" Cinema the "last word" in an endeavour to give its patrons high-class entertainment in complete comfort, and a perusal of this programme giving particulars of its construction and policy will convince readers that everything possible has been done for their benefit.

The Directors fully realise the remarkable progress that has been and is still being made in the Cinematograph World, and all the latest and most up-to-date Western Electric apparatus for the projection of talking pictures has been installed in this Theatre.

The Association

Mr. J. C. Donada, the Managing Director of the "Regal," for 20 years a prominent member of the famous Paramount organization, has promised his patrons the best pictures, perfect talkies and first-class music, a claim made possible by the fact that the "Regal" is associated with the new all-British cinema controlling organization known as County Cinemas, Ltd., which enjoys a unique position in the Cinematograph industry.

Patrons will therefore appreciate that it will be quite unnecessary for them to have to undertake a tiresome journey to town, when, within a short distance from their own homes, they can enjoy in luxury and comfort all the most recent film productions, presented in the finest possible manner.

149

THE DIRECTORS believe that service to the public is as important as providing the very best pictures, and Mr. A. E. Warren, who is directing the opening of this new luxurious Cinema, is a firm believer in service. "REGAL SERVICE IS ROYAL" will be our slogan also.

Mr. Warren has had a wide experience at managing both stage and cinema theatres, and it is as a result of this life-long association with the theatre that he is now more convinced than ever that service plays a very important part.

After a visit to Australia, Mr. Warren joined Mr. C. J. Donada and the County Cinema Group, and he re-organised the Majestic Cinema, Wembley, and the Regal at Beckenham. He also opened the Plaza Cinema in Piccadilly, and Madame Tussauds Cinema, and Capitol, Cardiff.

Service is courtesy and courtesy is only kindliness, politeness and civility, but it is the keystone upon which this business is built.

Therefore it behoves every man and woman on the theatre staff to remember it always, and to treat all patrons with courtesy and careful consideration. As is pointed out to the staff - kindness, and courtesy, is infectious.

Courtesy may become a trade mark - it is the magnet which draws, and holds, loyal patrons. A Theatre attracts for the entertainment, the plea-sure it will give. There can be no entertainment, no pleasure, no feeling of contentment, where courtesy is lacking. Courtesy, good cheer, friendliness, the ability to serve without ostentation, the willingness to give freely of that spirit of welcome that warms the heart - this makes friends of patrons and boosters of those who pass through our doors. Patrons of places of amusement come to forget their workaday worries, and that is why we always impress upon our staff that they are acting as a host and that they should conduct themselves as if they were in their own home.

For the REGAL (KINGSTON), LTD.,
      A. H. REED, Chairman.
      C. J. DONADA Managing Director.
      A. WRIGHT.
      J. W. HOWE

The Regal's Organist

A Few Personal Notes about
REGINALD FOORT, F.R.C.O., A.R.C.M.
The Famous Broadcasting and Recording Organist

REGINALD FOORT was born at Daventry and played the piano in public at the age of seven, and had his first organ post at the age of twelve. Later on he went to the Royal College of Music to study with Sir Walter Parratt. He obtained his F.R.C.O. Diploma at the age of seventeen and the same year was appointed organist and choirmaster at St. Mary's Church, Bryanston Square, W.

During the war he served for nearly five years in the Royal Navy and was present at the battle of Jutland. Some years after the war he gave up his church appointment and turned his attention to the cinema organ.

In those days, just as at present, there existed a kind of vicious circle. It was not possible to get a job as a cinema organist until one had had experience, and one could not get experience until one had a job. Mr. Foort solved this problem in rather a curious way. In London all the cinemas are open seven days a week, but there is a strict rule that everyone employed in a cinema must have one day a week free. So he arranged a circuit of deputising and for four months played in a different cinema every day on the regular man's day off. "At the end of this time," says Mr. Foort, "I really believe I knew all there was to know about accompanying pictures. It was a terribly hard method of getting experience, but I have never regretted it, as the only way to know all about any job is to tackle it from the bottom."

He was then offered and accepted his first position as a regular solo organist at the New Picture House, Edinburgh, where a Wurlitzer was being installed. He had had no Wurlitzer experience, but was counting on getting a few days' practice before having to open the organ. Unfortunately, when he arrived in Edinburgh the organ was not finished and he was unable to start practising on it until the Saturday night at midnight and the opening ceremony was fixed for the Monday at noon with every celebrity in the city invited to be present. So he sat down at the organ and practised all night on the Saturday night, went home to breakfast and a few hours' sleep on the Sunday morning and spent the rest of the Sunday practising. The opening ceremony was a great success.

Nine weeks later he was transferred to the New Gallery, where he very rapidly became famous through his broadcast recitals and gramophone records. He was, of course, the pioneer of cinema organ records and some of the records he made on the New Gallery organ still command quite a considerable sale. Later on he went to Paris to open the Paramount Theatre, came back to the Palladium when it was converted into a cinema and then opened the Empire, Leicester Square. He then went to the Regent Theatre, Bournemouth, where his broadcasting was particularly successful.

He has just completed a year's engagement at the Regal, Marble Arch, and we feel sure that patrons of the "Regal" Theatre, Kingston, will be as delighted as we are that we have succeeded in persuading him to accept the appointment of organist at this theatre.

When he has had a few weeks to settle down in the new appointment, Mr. Foort hopes to begin a new series of broadcast recitals from the "Regal" Theatre, Kingston. He is simply delighted with the very fine three-manual Wurlitzer which has been installed in this theatre, and he is hoping to use it in the near future for making some of the finest gramophone records he has ever made in his life.

The Organ
The "Regal" Organ is a mighty voiced Wurlitzer Hope-Jones Unit Orchestra which combines the world's finest pipe organ with all the different voices of the symphony orchestra under the control of one musician. There is no other organ in the world which presents such an instrumentation. It is the immediate response together with special characteristic voicing for theatre work made possible by the Wurlitzer Unit System and enabling the organist to play in quick time, that marks the great point of difference between the Wurlitzer and organs built along straight organ lines. It is possible to play any kind of music and especially that which requires rapid technique and quick response that has never been possible of proper performance on the straight organ.

There is nothing in the entire gamut of human emotion that cannot be expressed musically on a Wurlitzer better than on any other instrument or group of instruments. The Wurlitzer Unit Orchestra contains inventions of Robert Hope-Jones of Liverpool, who is known throughout the musical world as the master organ builder of all times and is credited with nine-tenths of the innovations in the organ during the last twenty years. It is the wonderful range of tone colour that proves such a fascination with organists and causes them to prefer playing a Wurlitzer to a straight organ.

152

The Expressive power of the Wurlitzer Hope-Jones Unit Orchestra must be heard to be believed. Another feature which is of the deepest import, is that enabling the organist to obtain expression from his finger-touch. By means of the Hope-Jones "Double Touch" any particular note or notes can be brought out above the remainder of the organ, and this without raising the hands from the keyboard. To each keyboard are fitted two distinct touches, the first playing the stops that are drawn on the first touch stop keys, and the second touch, which is made by a little extra pressure, the stop or stops drawn on the second touch stop keys are brought into use. The two touches are absolutely distinct from each other, and no mistake can be made by bringing the second touch into action when it is not needed.

The "pizzicato touch" is also a very valuable adjunct by means of which the staccato or plucking effect (similar to a violinist plucking the strings of his violin with his fingers) can be obtained on specific stops arranged for the purpose. This is a most useful and wonderful accessory and enables the organist to obtain results impossible through any other medium. With these means of finger touch expression a performer with the one hand could be playing upon the flute and by depressing certain fingers a little harder the melody could be brought out on the Clarinet and at the same time have the Oboe Horn playing pizzicato. This is all accomplished with the fingers of one hand, and shows the possibilities of our instrument over those of other makes.

The Electro-pneumatic action is absolutely reliable, as it has stood the test of time, having been used in organs for over thirty years. It is instantaneous in attack, and is capable of far faster repetition than is possible with the human hand. All the contacts in these instruments are made with sterling silver, which, after exhaustive tests, has proved to be the best method for the purpose. Sterling silver is of course very expensive, but the results obtained justify its use. The wind pressures in the Wurlitzer Unit Organ are considerably higher than those used by other builders. By this means unlimited power is obtained, without the loss of any of the mellowness of tone, which is due to the Wurlitzer scientific methods of voicing.

The Wurlitzer Unit Organ contains all the tones usually found in the Church organ combined with such orchestral instruments as Clarinet, Flute, Piccolo, Violins, Cornets, Trombones, Saxophones, etc. In addition to those are to be found the Vox Humana, refined Musical Sleigh Bells, Harps, Xylophones, Cathedral Chimes, Orchestral Bells, Vibrating Bells, Bass, Kettle, and Snare Drum, Tambourines,

Triangles, Castanets, and a host of other instruments, in fact every musical instrument and accessory of which a symphony is composed. The entire instrument is operated by one musician from a console or keyboard placed in the orchestra pit or in any location desired.

THE UNION CINEMAS COMPTON SPECIAL 2-MANUAL 4-UNIT ORGAN

PEDAL

Tromba	16
Tibia	16
Tromba	8
Tibia	8
Gamba	8
Flute	8

Bass Drum Tap - f
Bass Drum Tap - p
Bass Drum Roll
Snare Drum
Cymbal Tap
Cymbal Crash
Triangle
Accompaniment to Pedal
Solo to Pedal
Four adjustable toe pistons

ACCOMPANIMENT

Contra Gamba .	T.C.16
Tromba	8
Tibia	8
Gamba	8
Flute	8
Tromba	4
Tibia	4

Gamba	4
Flute	4
Twelfth (Flute) . .	.2²/₃
Gambette	2
Flautino . . .	2
Marimba	8
Vibraphone . . .	4

Snare Drum
Castanets
Tambourine
Chinese Block
Tom Tom
Sleigh Bells
Sand Block
Second Touch:

Tromba	8
Tibia	4

Solo to Accompaniment
Six adjustable thumb pistons

SOLO

Tromba	16
Tibia	16
Contra Gamba . . .	T.C.16
Bourdon	T.C.16
Tromba	8

Tibia	8
Gamba	8
Concert Fluite . .	8
Tromba	4
Tibia	4
Gamba	4
Flute	4
Tibia Twelfth . . .	$2^2/_3$
Twelfth (Flute) . .	$2^2/_3$
Ocarina	2
Flautino	2
Tierce	$1^3/_5$
Xylophone	
Glockenspiel	
Orchestral Bells	
Melotone	8
Melotone	4
Melotone Twelfth .	$2^2/_3$
Super Melotone .	2
Krummhorn . .	8
Cor Anglais . .	8
Chimes	
Carillon	
Echo Control	
Glide	
Vibrato	
Sub Octave	
Super Octave	
Eight adjustable thumb pistons	

TREMULANTS
Tibia
Tromba - Flute - Gamba

BALANCED PEDALS
Organ
Melotone
General Crescendo

VENTILS (By stopkeys)
Tibia Treble
Tromba - Flute - Gamba
Basses
Percussions

EFFECTS, etc.
By stopkeys:
Surf
Aeroplane
By toe pistons:
Birds
Auto
Cymbal Roll
Snare Drum - Grand Crash
Cymbal Crash

Operator

LIGHTS (By stopkeys)
Off
Auto
Red
Blue
Green
Amber
Orange
Sky Blue
Turquoise
Mauve

156

THE UNION CINEMAS COMPTON SPECIAL 3-MANUAL 6-UNIT ORGAN

PEDAL

Acoustic Bass . .	32
Trombone . . .	16
Diaphone . . .	16
Tibia Bass . . .	16
Tromba	8
Diapason	8
Tibia	8
Strings II	8
Flute	8

Bass Drum Tap - f
Bass Drum Tap - p
Drum Roll
Snare Drum
Cymbal Tap
Cymbal Crash
Cymbal Roll
Triangle
Traps to Second Touch
Accompaniment to Pedal
Great to Pedal
Solo to Pedal

ACCOMPANIMENT

Strings II	T.C.16
Bourdon	T.C.16
Tromba	8
Diapason	8
Tibia	8
Krumet	8
Strings II . . .	8
Flute	8
Tromba	4
Octave	4
Tibia	4
Strings II . . .	4
Flute	4
Twelfth	$2^{2/3}$
Flautino	2
Marimba	8
Vibraphone . . .	4

Snare Drum
Castanets
Tambourine
Chinese Block
Sleigh Bells
Tom Tom
Sand Block
Octave
Second Touch:

Tromba	8
Diapason . . .	8

Tibia	8	Tibia	8
Great to Accompaniment .	4	Krumet	8
Solo to Accompaniment .	8	Strings II . . .	8
		Tromba	4
		Tibia	4

GREAT

Trombone	16	Xylophone	
Diaphone	16	Glockenspiel	
Tibia	16	Bells	
Strings II . . .	T.C.16	Melotone . . .	8
Tromba	8	Melotone . . .	4
Diapason	8	Melo Twelfth . .	$2^2/_3$
Tibia	8	Melo Fifteenth . .	2
Krumet	8	Krummhorn . . .	8
Strings II	8	Cor Anglais . . .	8
Flute	8	Musette	8
Tromba	4	Carillon	
Octave	4	Chimes	
Tibia	4	Echo Control 1	
Strings II	4	Echo Control 2	
Flute	4	Vibrato	
Tibia	$2^2/_3$	Melotone off	
Flute	$2^2/_3$	Suboctave	
Piccolo	2	Octave	
Fifteenth	2	Unison off	
Tierce	$1^3/_5$	Melotone off	
Xylophone			
Glockenspiel			
Bells			
Suboctave			
Octave			
Solo to Great . . .	16		
Solo to Great . . .	8		

TREMULANTS

Tibia
Diapason
Krumet - Tromba
Strings II - Flute

SOLO

Trombone . . .	16
Diaphone	16
Tibia	16
Krumet . . .	T.C.16
Trombone . . .	8
Diaphone	8

VENTILS (By stopkeys)

Tibia Treble
CC Diapason
CC Tibia - Krumet - Tromba
Strings II - Flute
CCC Tromba - Tibia - Xylophone -
Glockenspiel
Traps - CCC Diaphone

ACCESSORIES

8 adjustable thumb pistons to
  Accompaniment
8 adjustable thumb pistons to
  Great
8 adjustable thumb pistons to
  Solo
3 adjustable toe pistons to Pedal

EFFECTS, etc.

By stopkeys:
Surf
Aeroplane
By toe pistons:
Birds
Auto
Firebell
Siren
Cymbal Roll
Cymbal Crash
Snare Drum
Grand Crash

Operator

BALANCED PEDALS

Balanced Expression Pedal to Main
Balanced Expression Pedal to Solo
Balanced General Crescendo Pedal

LIGHTS (By stopkeys)

Off
Auto
Red
Blue
Green
Amber
Orange
Sky Blue
Turquoise
Mauve

INDEX